Easy Piano

Best of KELLY CLARKSON

ISBN 978-1-4234-3415-3

Hal•Leonard®
CORPORATION
7777 W. BLUEMOUND RD. P.O. BOX 13819 MILWAUKEE, WI 53213

Visit Hal Leonard Online at
www.halleonard.com

ADDICTED

Words and Music by KELLY CLARKSON,
DAVID HODGES and BEN MOODY

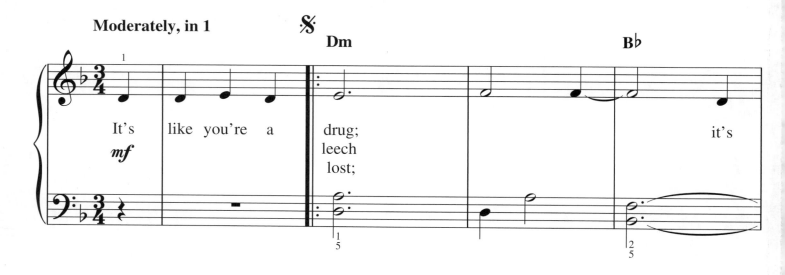

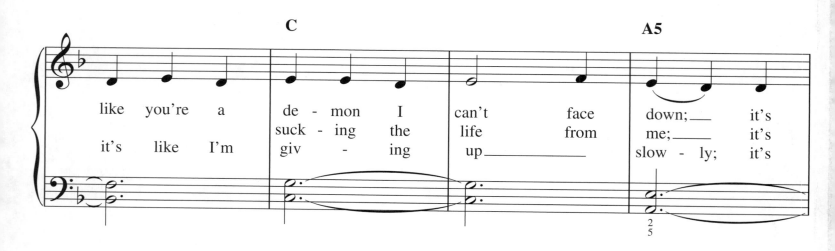

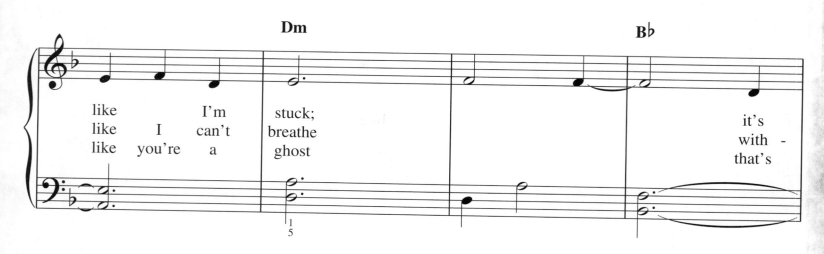

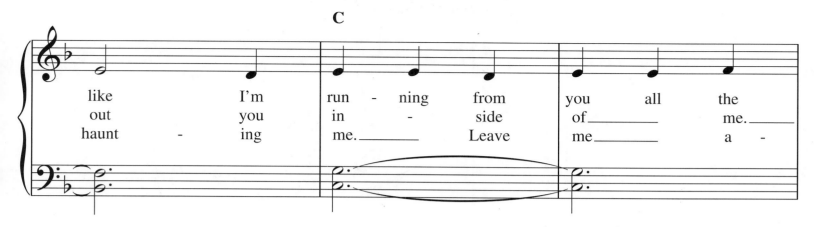
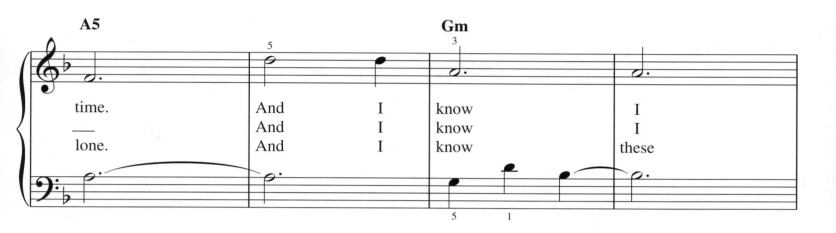
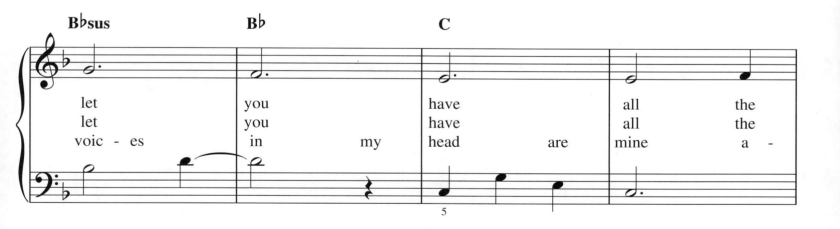
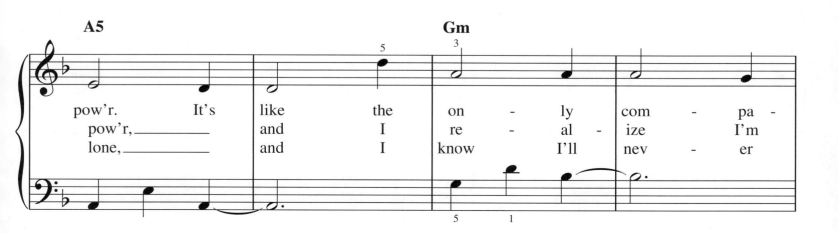

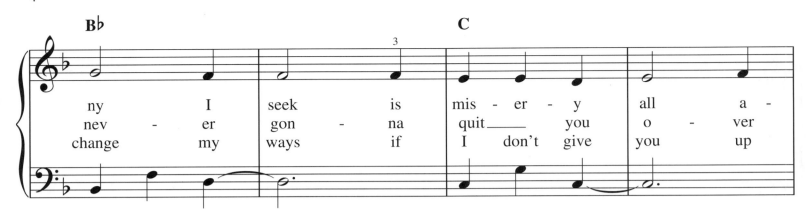

ny   I   seek   is   mis - er - y   all   a -
nev - er   gon - na   quit___ you   o - ver
change my   ways   if   I   don't give   you   up

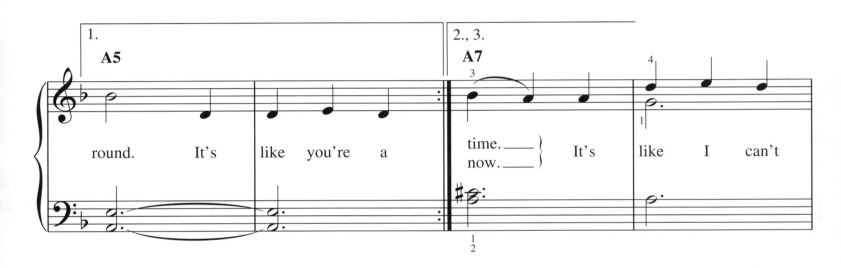

round.   It's   like you're   a   time.___ | now.___   It's   like   I   can't

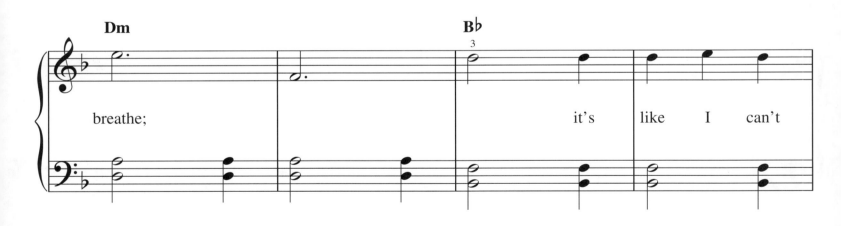

breathe;   it's   like   I   can't

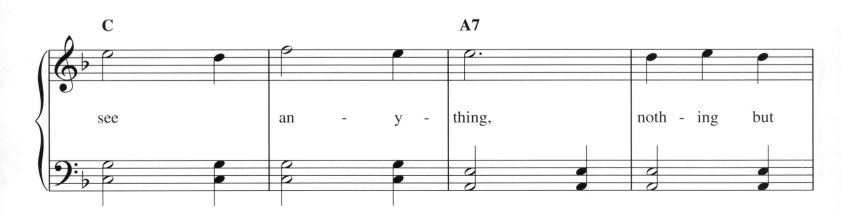

see   an - y - thing,   noth - ing but

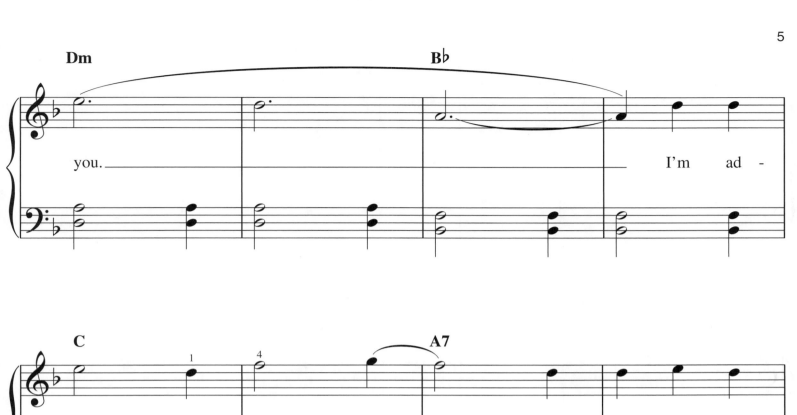

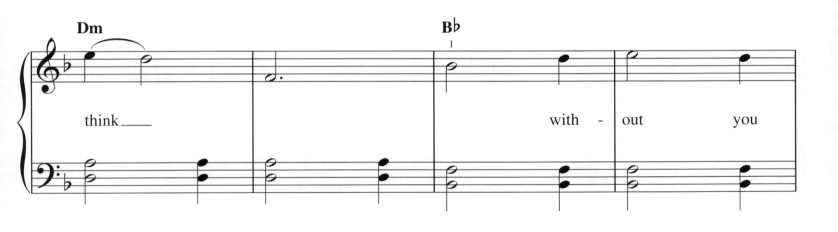

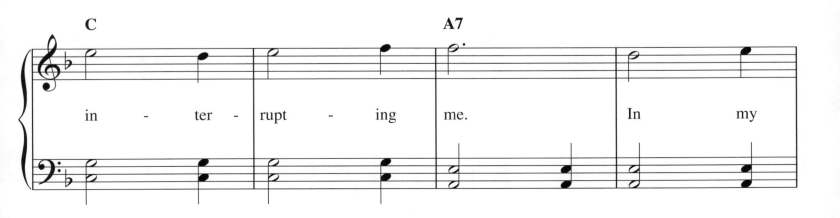

thoughts,___ in my dreams,___ you've

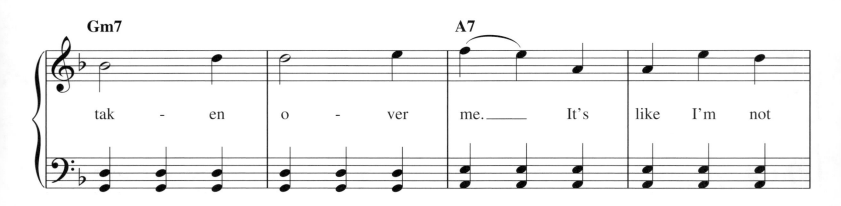

tak - en o - ver me.___ It's like I'm not

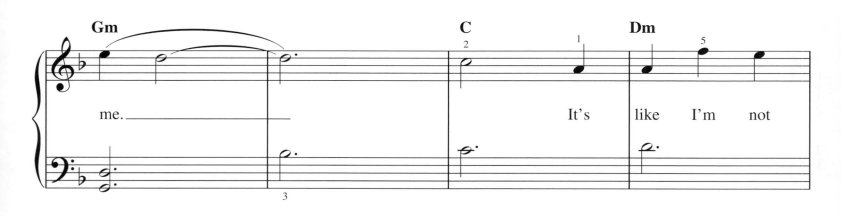

me.___ It's like I'm not

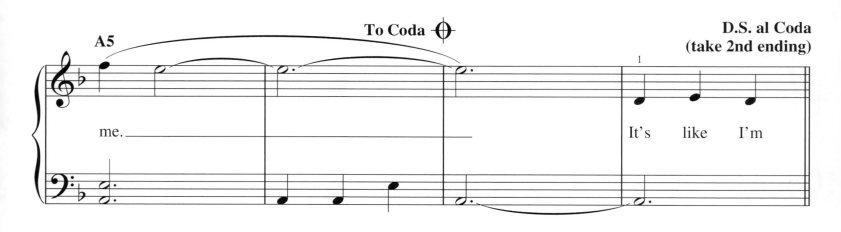

me.___ It's like I'm

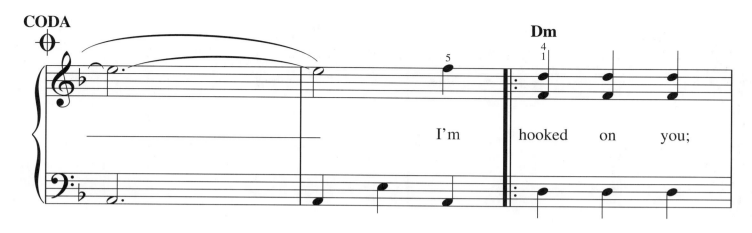

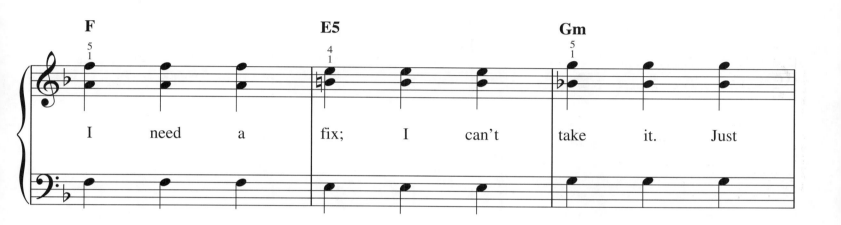

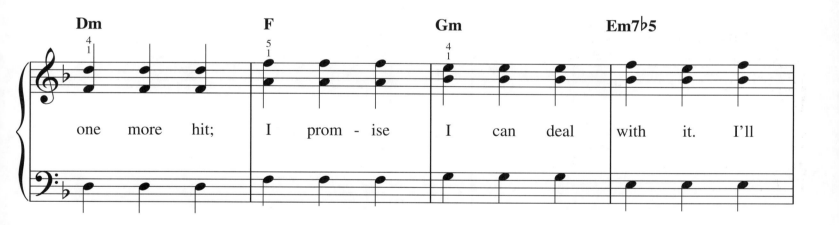

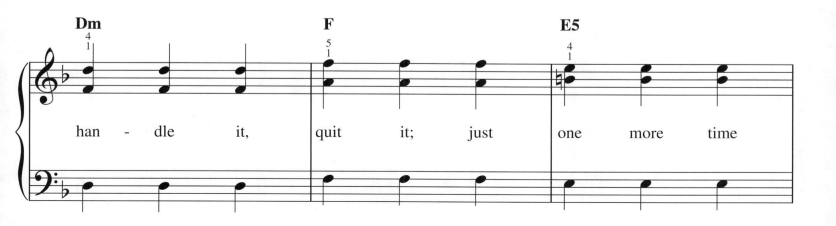

8

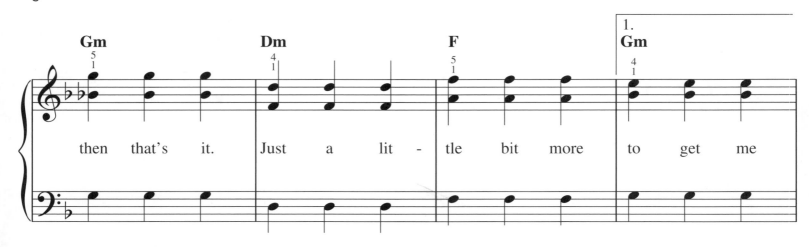

then that's it. Just a lit - tle bit more to get me

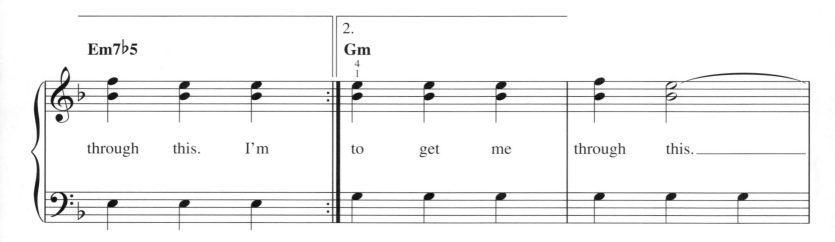

through this. I'm to get me through this.___

___ It's like I can't breathe;

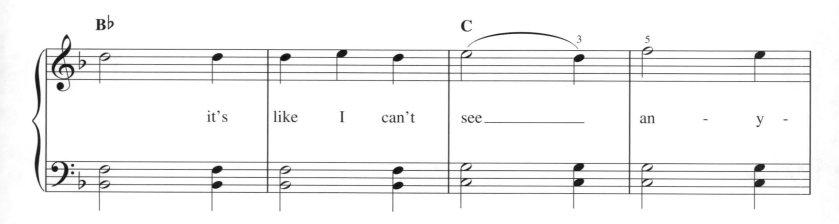

it's like I can't see___ an - y -

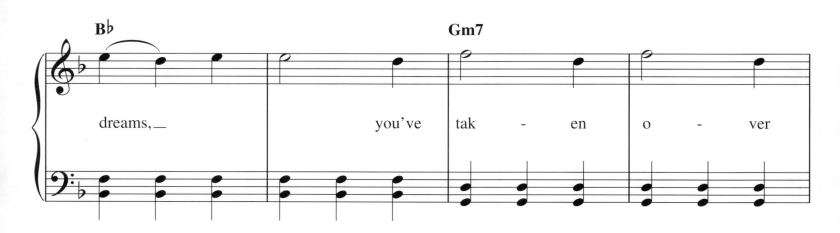

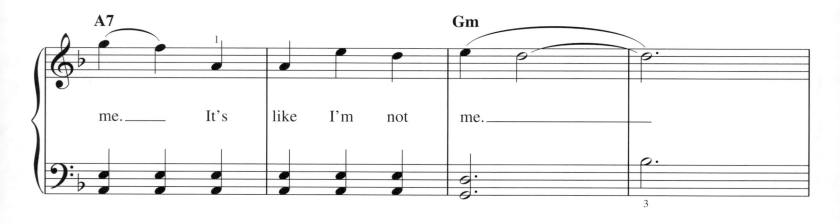

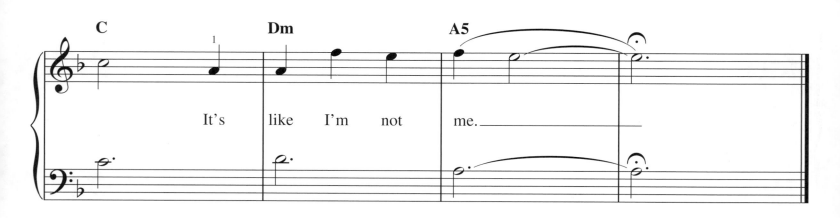

BE STILL

Words and Music by KELLY CLARKSON
and ABEN EUBANKS

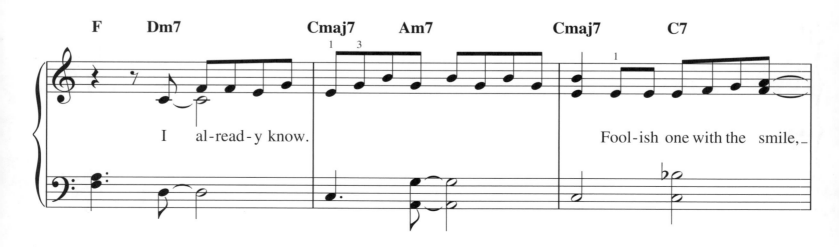

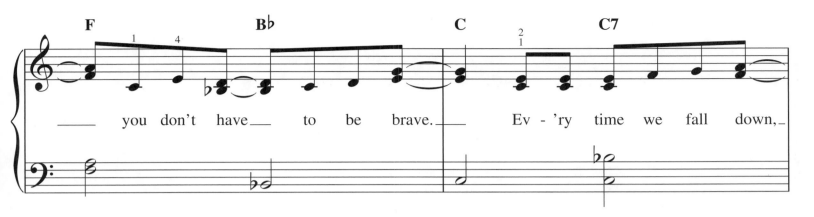

you don't have___ to be brave.___ Ev-'ry time we fall down,___

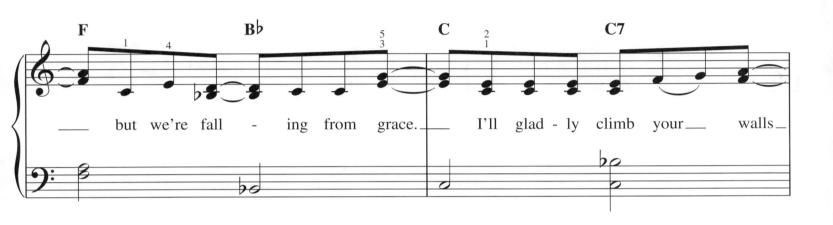

but we're fall - ing from grace.___ I'll glad-ly climb your___ walls___

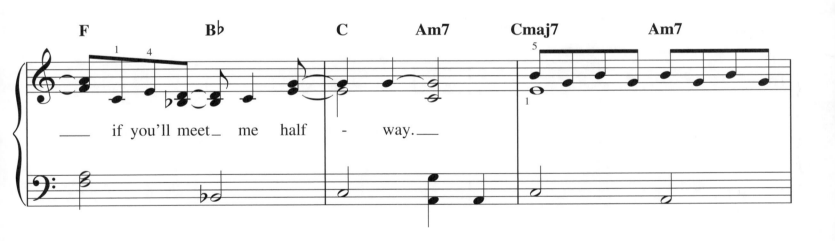

if you'll meet___ me half - way.___

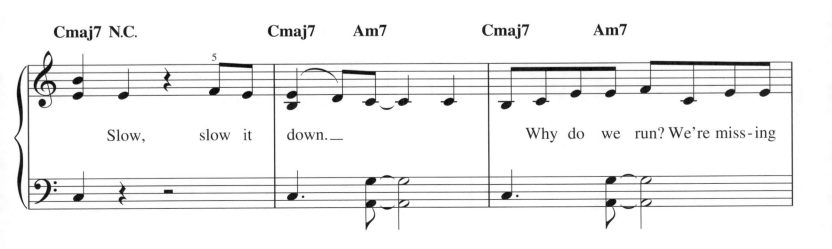

Slow, slow it down.___ Why do we run? We're miss-ing

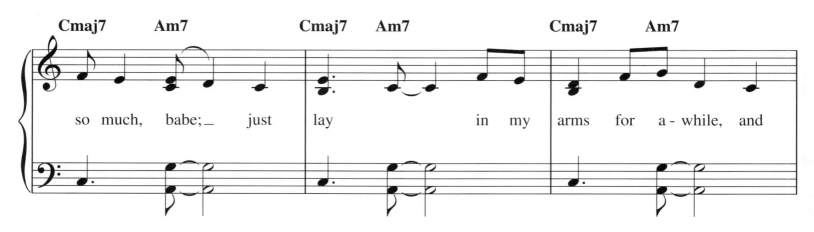

so much, babe;___ just lay in my arms for a-while, and

be still;___ we should-'ve known.

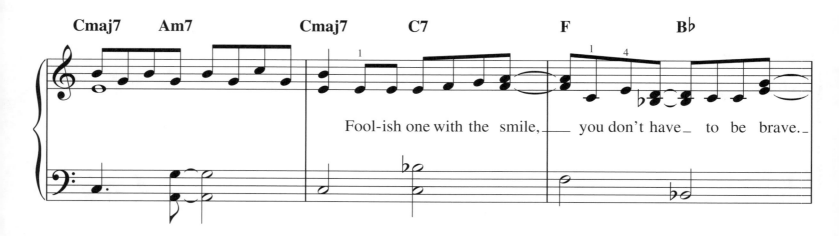

Fool-ish one with the smile,___ you don't have___ to be brave.___

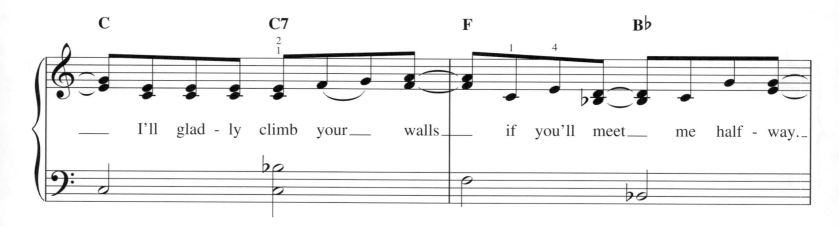

___ I'll glad-ly climb your___ walls___ if you'll meet___ me half-way.___

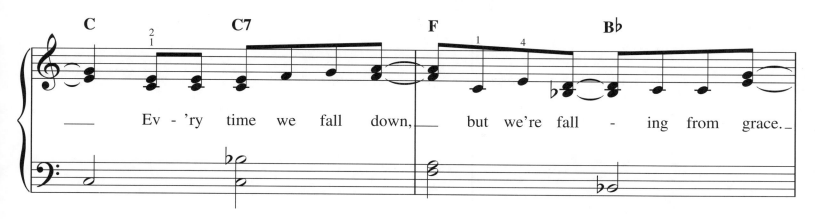

Ev - 'ry time we fall down,___ but we're fall - ing from grace.___

___ Here's my hand and my heart;___ it's yours___ to

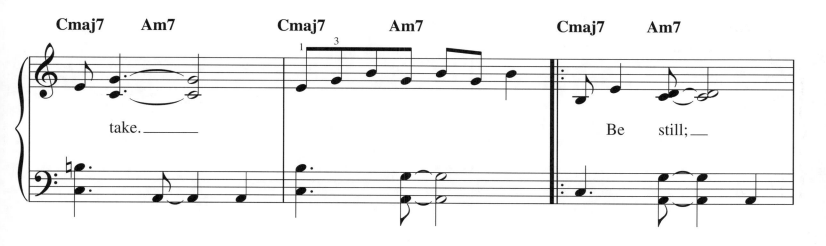

take._____ Be still;___

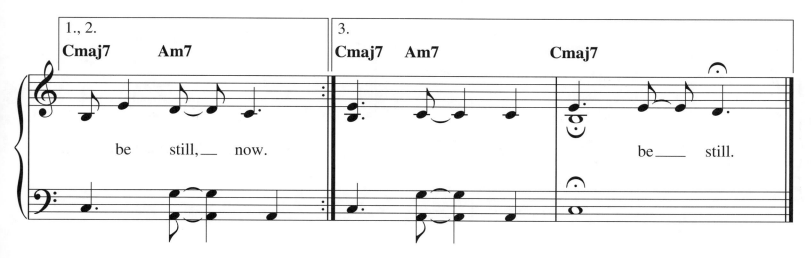

be still,___ now. be ___ still.

BEAUTIFUL DISASTER

Words and Music by REBECCA JOHNSON
and MATTHEW WILDER

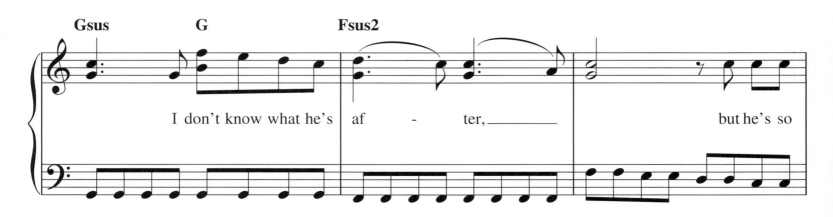

I don't know what he's af - ter,_____ but he's so

beau - ti - ful,_____ such a beau-ti-ful dis - as - ter._____

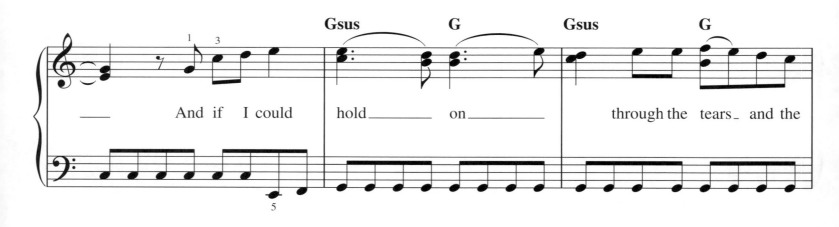

_____ And if I could hold_____ on_____ through the tears_ and the

laugh - ter,_____ would it be beau - ti - ful,_____

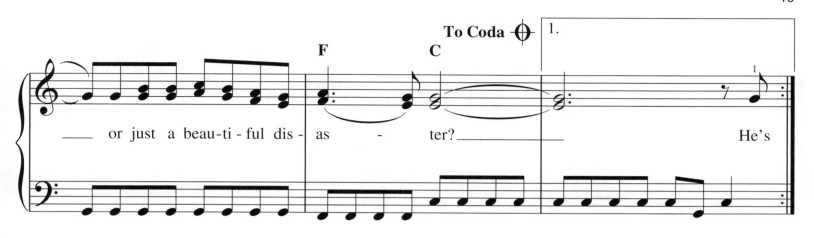

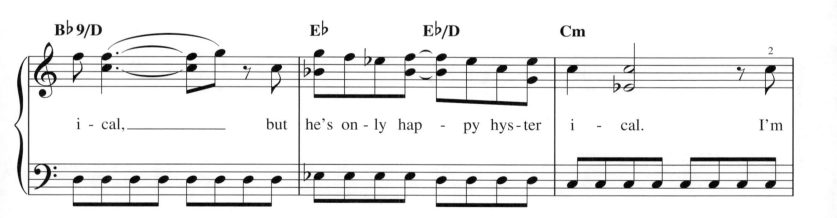

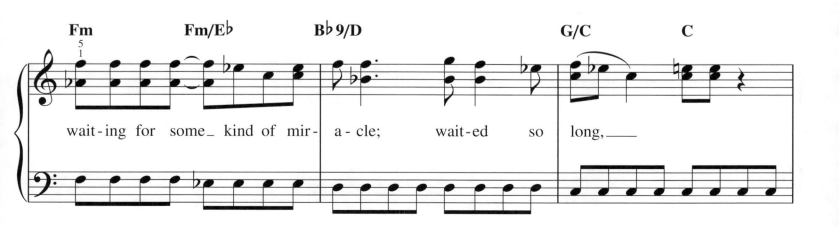

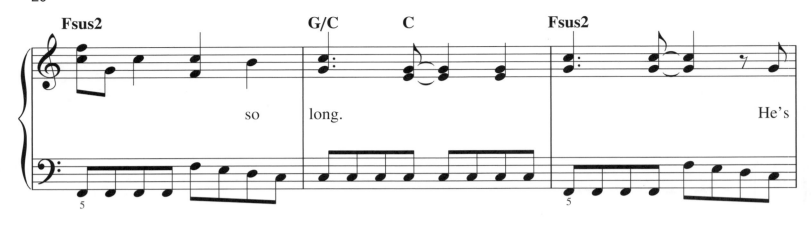

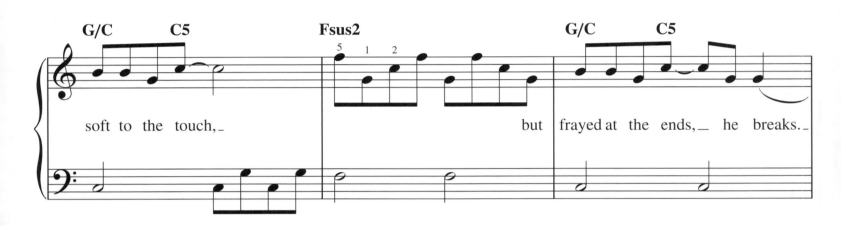

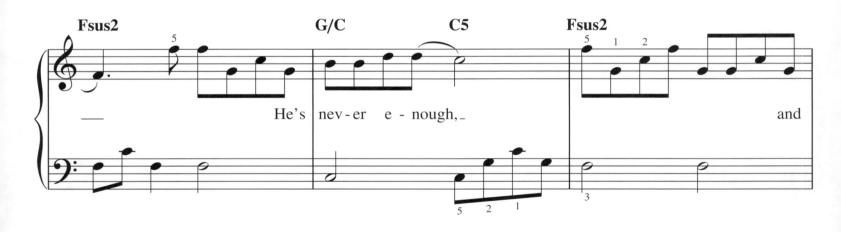

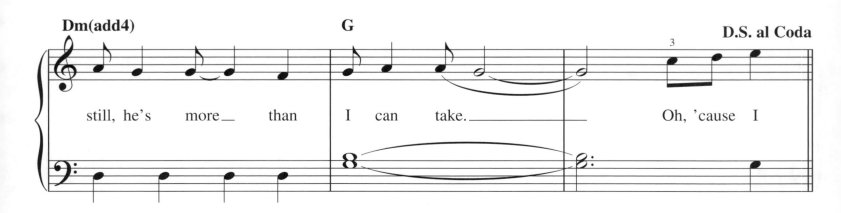

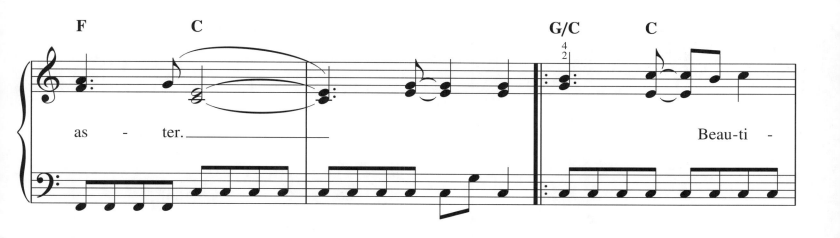

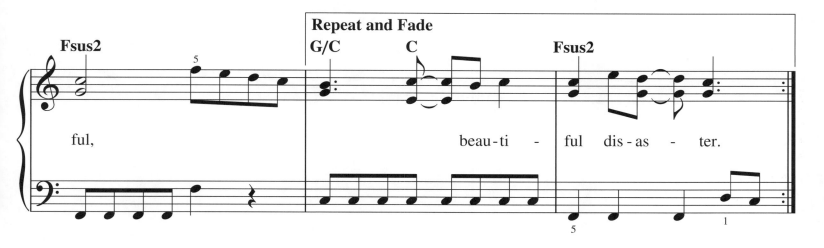

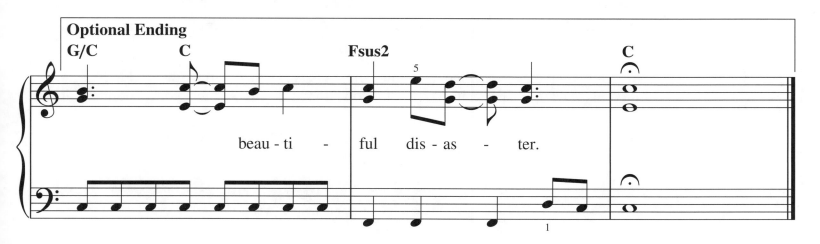

BECAUSE OF YOU

Words and Music by KELLY CLARKSON,
DAVID HODGES and BEN MOODY

Moderately slow

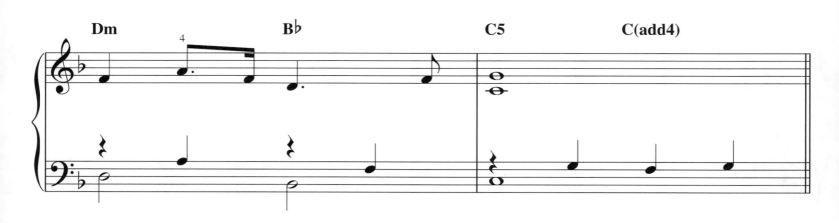

I will not make the same mis- takes_ that you did. I_____
I lose my way, and it's not too long_ be - fore you point_ it

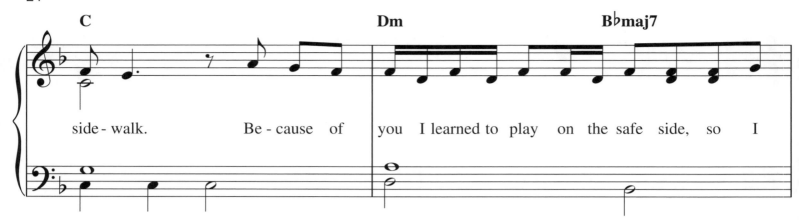

side - walk. Be - cause of you I learned to play on the safe side, so I

don't get hurt. Be - cause of you I find it hard to trust not on - ly

me, but ev -'ry - one a - round me. Be - cause of you I am a -

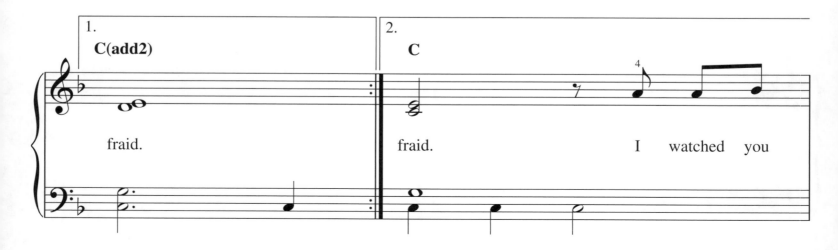

1.
fraid.

2.
fraid. I watched you

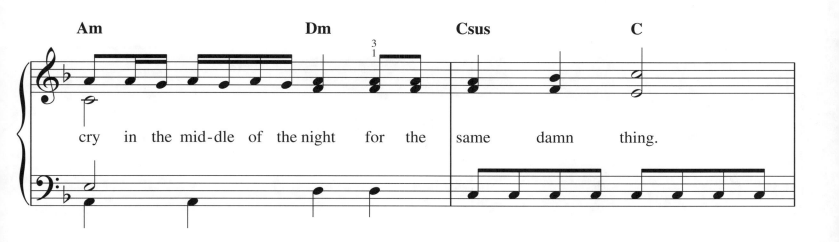

Be - cause of you I nev - er stray ___ too far from the

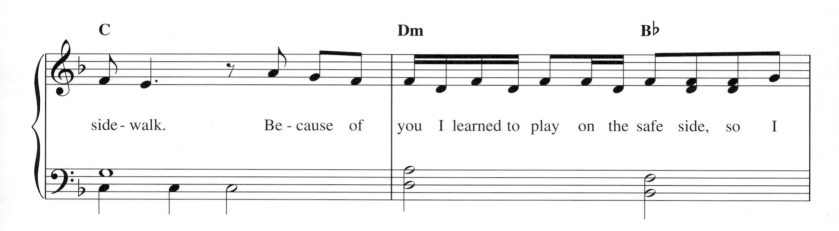

side - walk. Be - cause of you I learned to play on the safe side, so I

don't get hurt. Be - cause of you I try my hard - est just to for - get

ev - 'ry - thing. Be - cause of you I don't know how to let an - y - one

else in. Be - cause of you I'm a - shamed of my life, be - cause it's

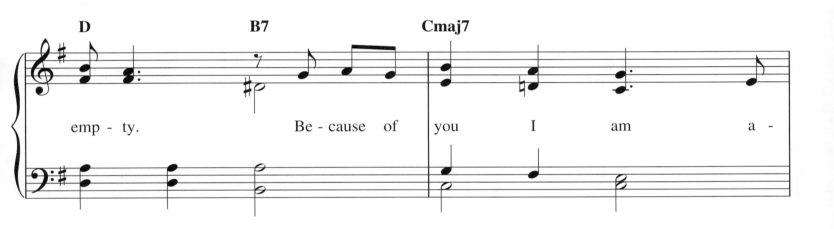

emp - ty. Be - cause of you I am a -

fraid. Be - cause of you, be - cause of

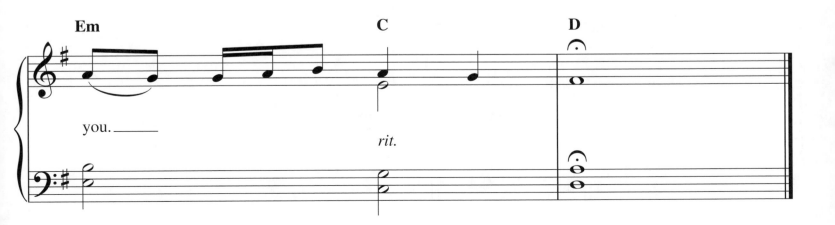

you. _____ *rit.*

BEHIND THESE HAZEL EYES

Words and Music by KELLY CLARKSON,
MARTIN SANDBERG and LUKASZ GOTTWALD

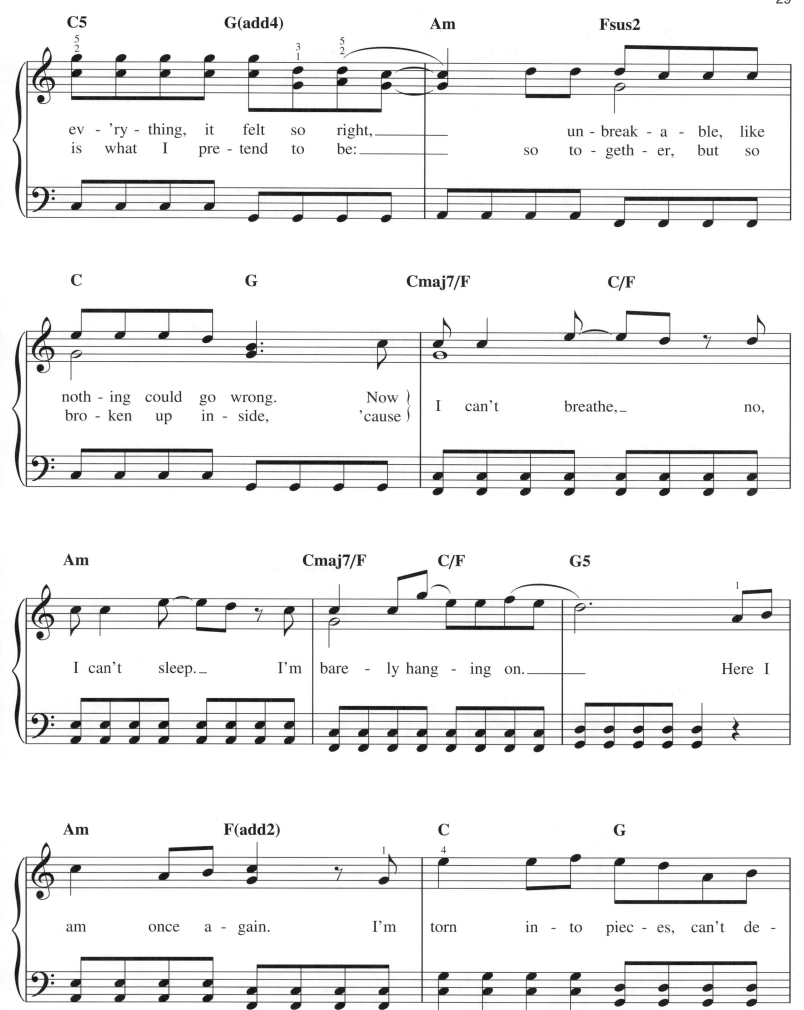

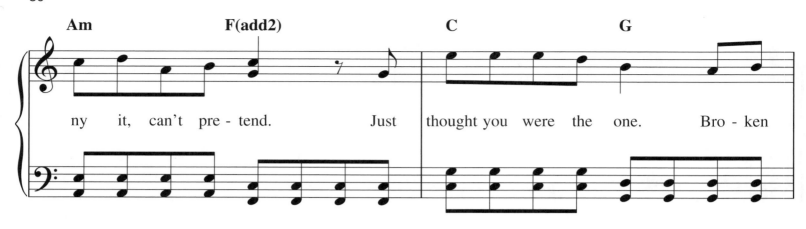

ny it, can't pre - tend. Just thought you were the one. Bro - ken

up deep in - side, but you won't get to see the tears I

cry be - hind these ha - zel eyes.

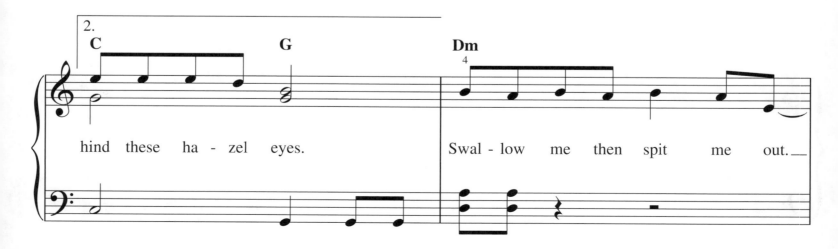

hind these ha - zel eyes. Swal - low me then spit me out.

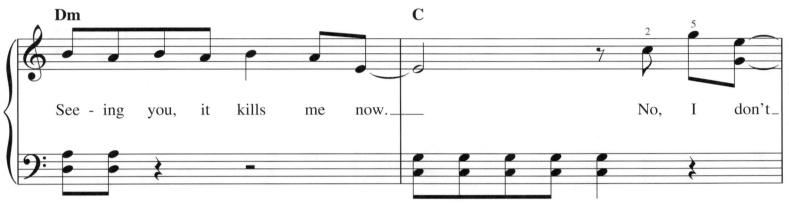

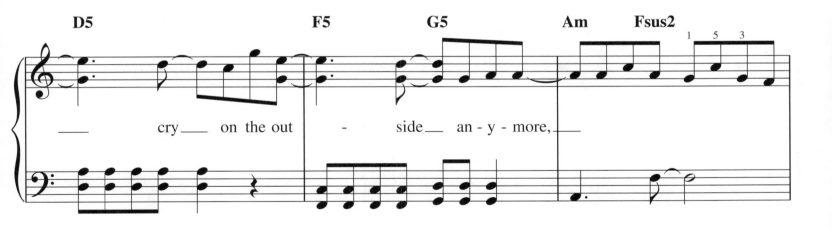

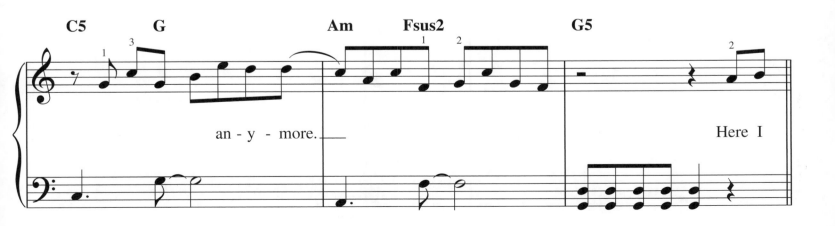

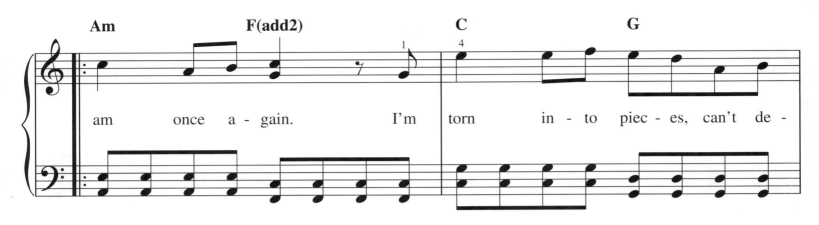

am once a-gain. I'm torn in-to piec-es, can't de-

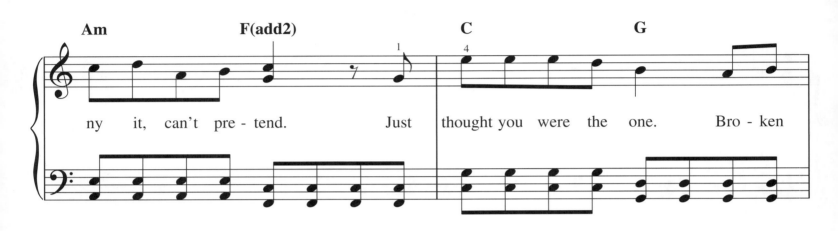

ny it, can't pre-tend. Just thought you were the one. Bro-ken

up deep in-side, but you won't get to see the tears I

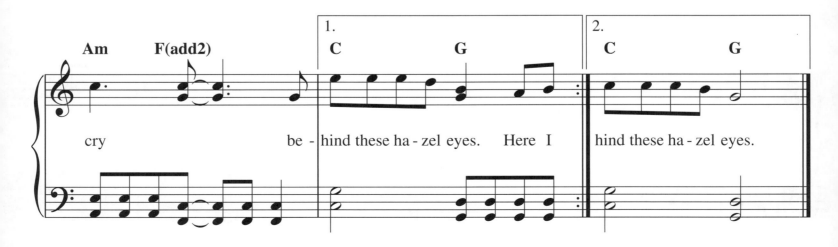

cry be-hind these ha-zel eyes. Here I hind these ha-zel eyes.

BREAKAWAY
from THE PRINCESS DIARIES 2: ROYAL ENGAGEMENT

Words and Music by BRIDGET BENENATE,
AVRIL LAVIGNE and MATTHEW GERRARD

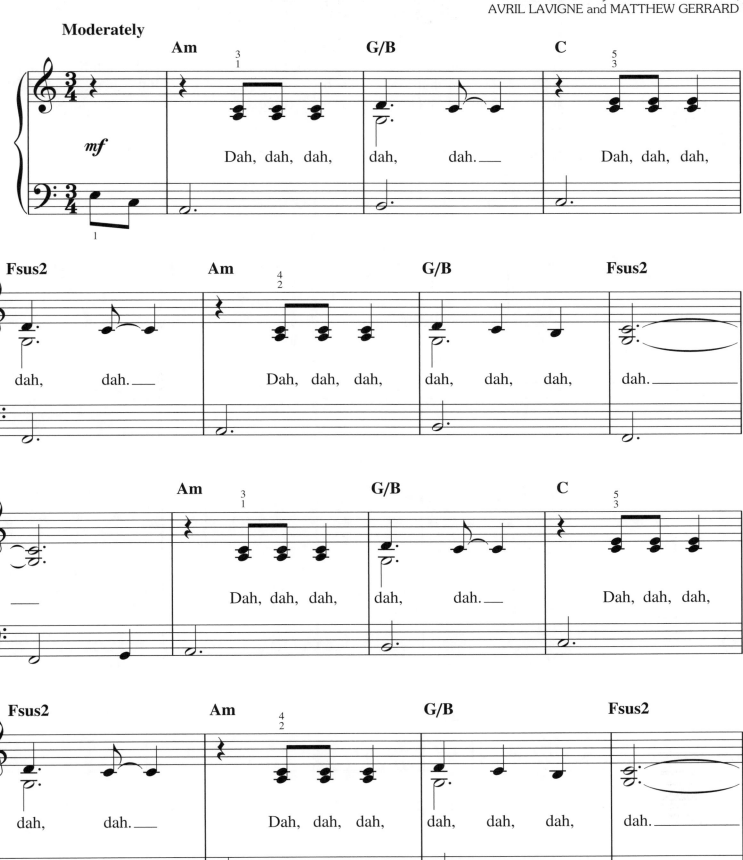

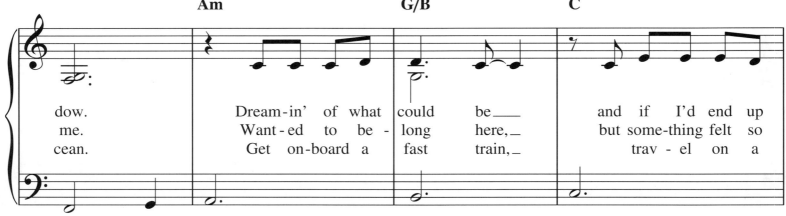

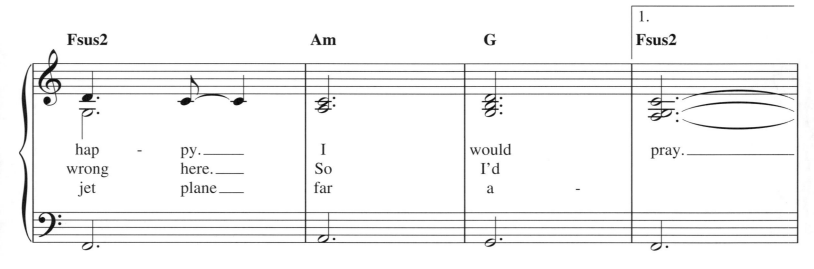

sky.   I'll___   make a wish.   Take a chance.   Make a change

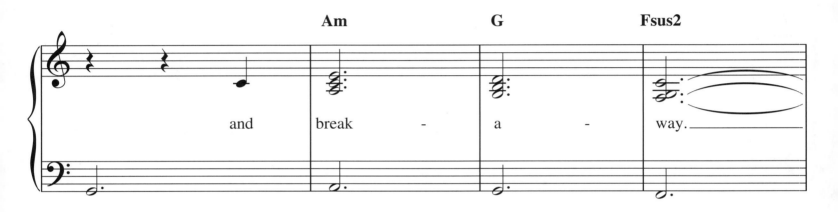

and   break - a - way.___

___   Out of the   dark-ness and   in-to the

sun,   but I won't for-   get all the   ones that I

love. I'll____ take a risk. Take a chance. Make a change

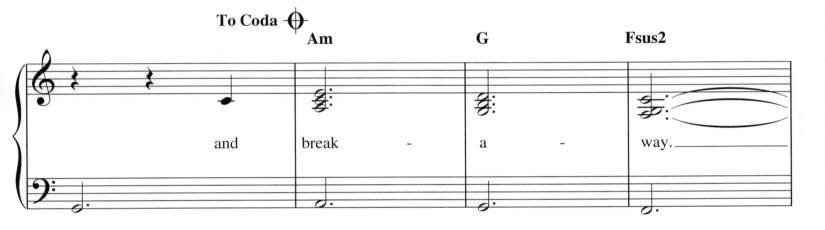

and break - a - way.____

____ Dah, dah, dah, dah, dah.____ Dah, dah, dah,

dah, dah.____ Dah, dah, dah, dah, dah, dah, dah.____

38

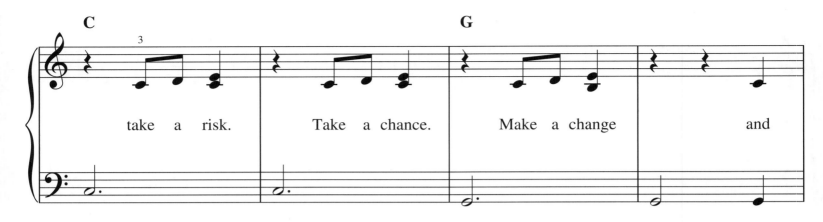

take a risk. Take a chance. Make a change and

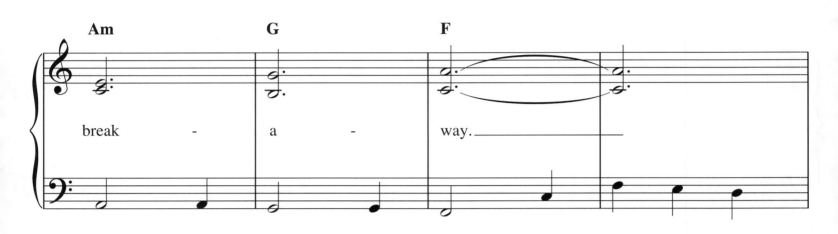

break - a - way.

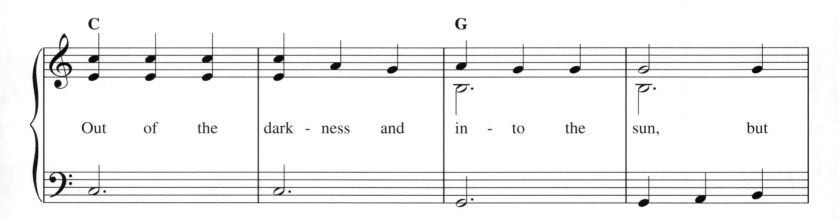

Out of the dark - ness and in - to the sun, but

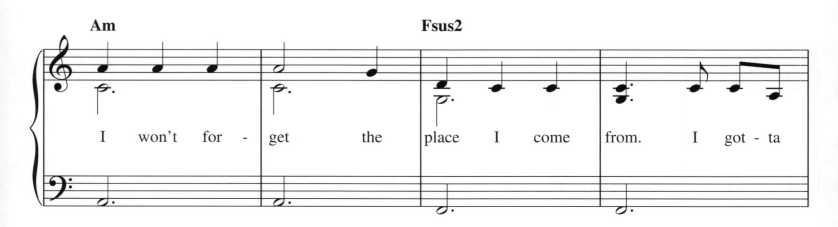

I won't for - get the place I come from. I got - ta

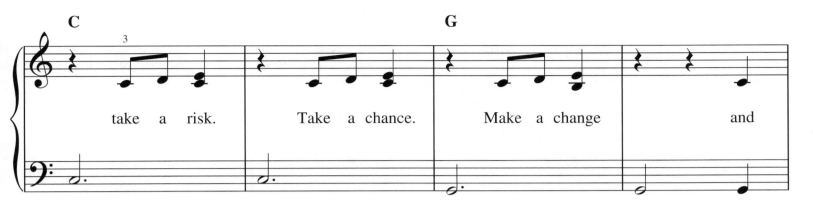

take a risk. Take a chance. Make a change and

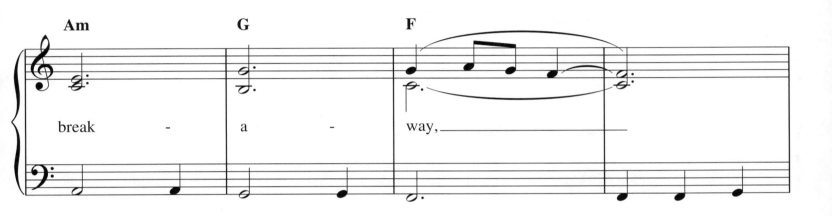

break - a - way,_____

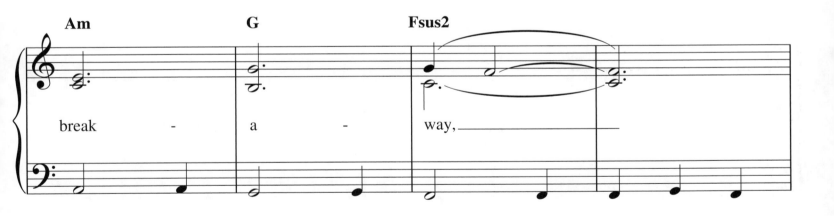

break - a - way,_____

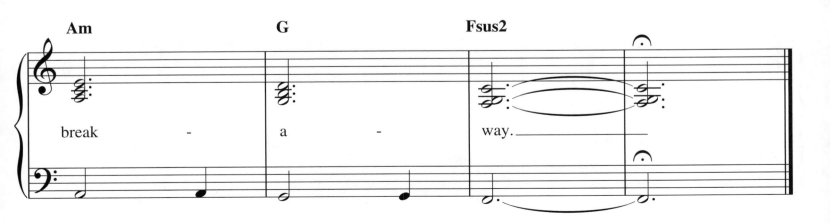

break - a - way._____

GONE

Words and Music by JOHN SHANKS
and KARA DioGUARDI

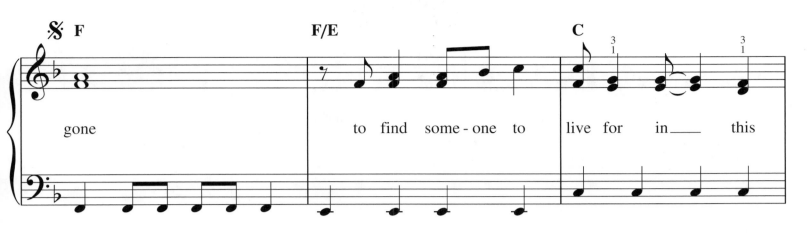

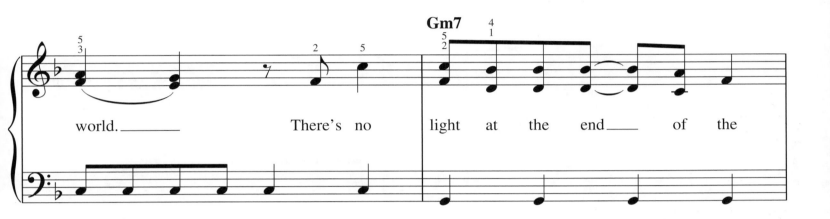

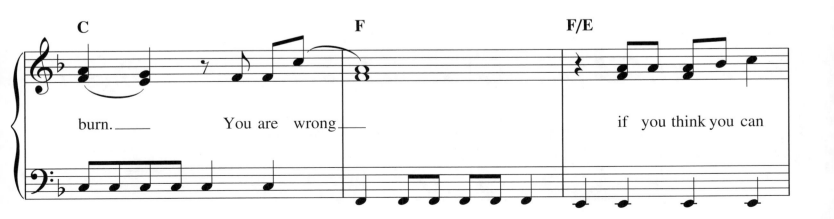

walk right through_ my door._____ That is just so you,_ com-ing

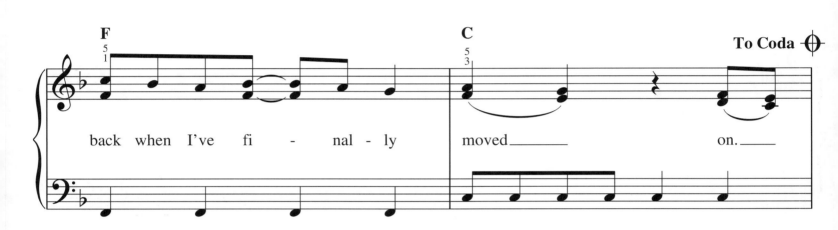

back when I've fi - nal-ly moved_____ on.____

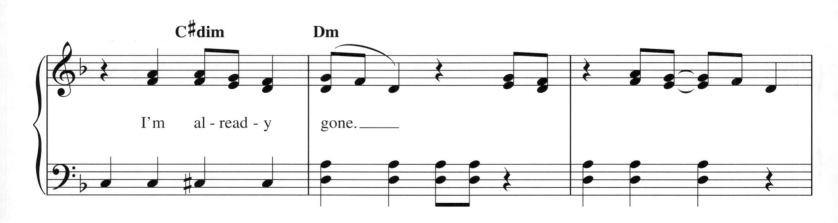

I'm al - read - y gone.____

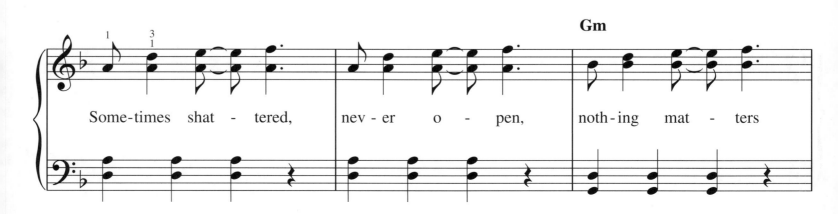

Some-times shat - tered, nev - er o - pen, noth-ing mat - ters

when you're bro - ken: That was me___ when - ev - er I___ was with

you. Al - ways end - ing, al - ways

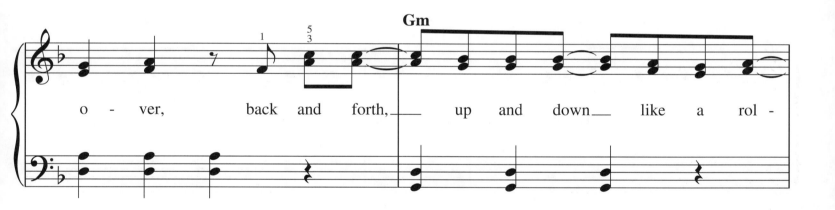

o - ver, back and forth,___ up and down___ like a rol -

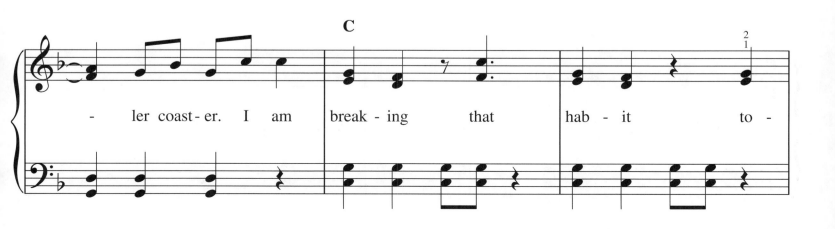

- ler coast - er. I am break - ing that hab - it to -

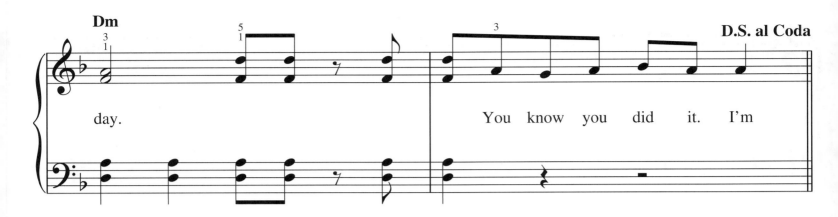

day.　　　　　You know you did it. I'm

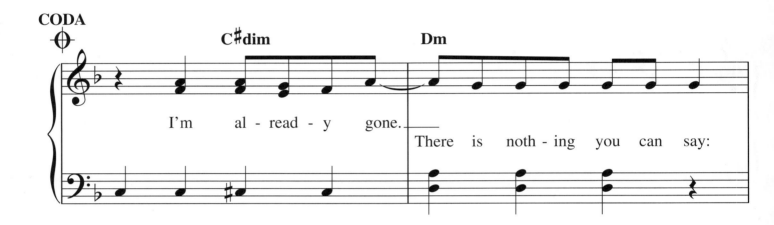

I'm al - read - y gone.　There is noth - ing you can say:

"Sor - ry" does - n't cut it, babe.　Take the hit and walk a - way,___

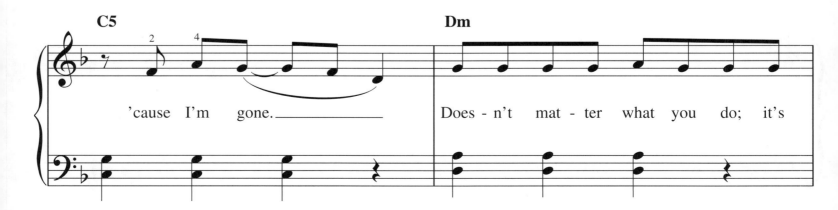

'cause I'm gone.___　Does - n't mat - ter what you do; it's

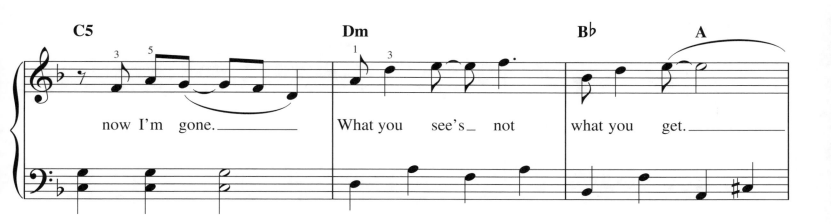

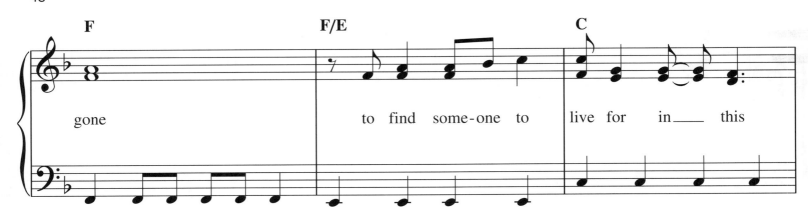

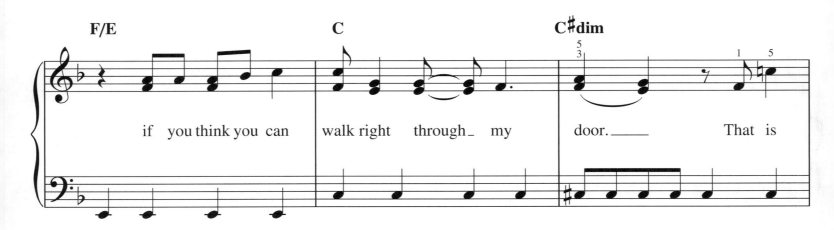

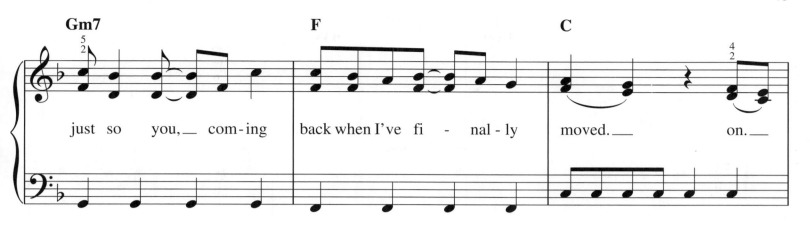

just so you,__ com-ing back when I've fi - nal-ly moved.__ on.__

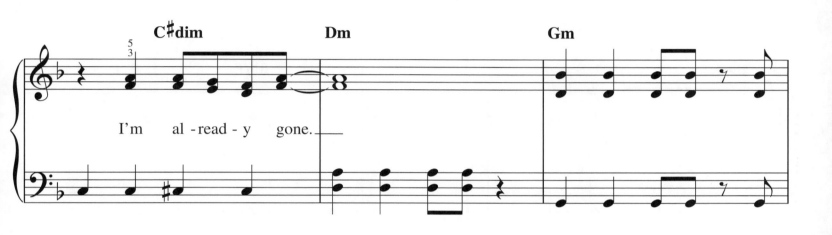

I'm al -read - y gone.__

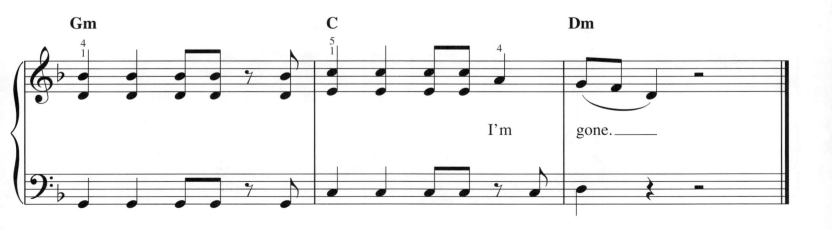

I'm gone._____

LOW

Words and Music by
JIMMY HARRY

Ev -'ry - bod - y's talk - in', _____ but they don't say a ____ thing.

____ They look at me with sad ___ eyes, but I don't want the

sym - pa - thy. It's cool you did - n't want ___ me.

Some-times you can't go back.

Why'd you have to go and make a mess like that?

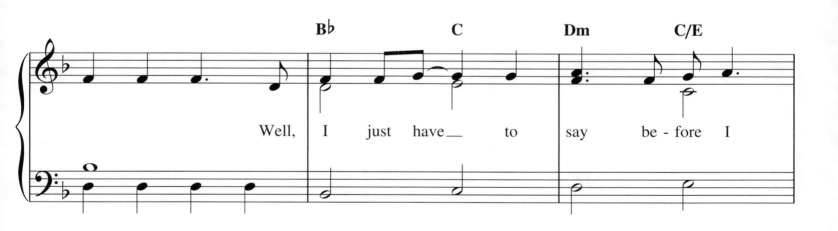

Well, I just have to say be-fore I

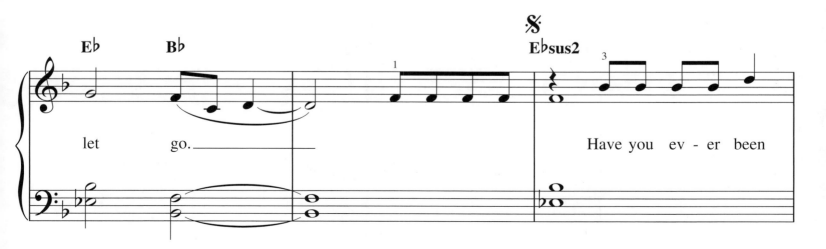

let go. Have you ev - er been

52

low? Have you ev - er had a friend that let you

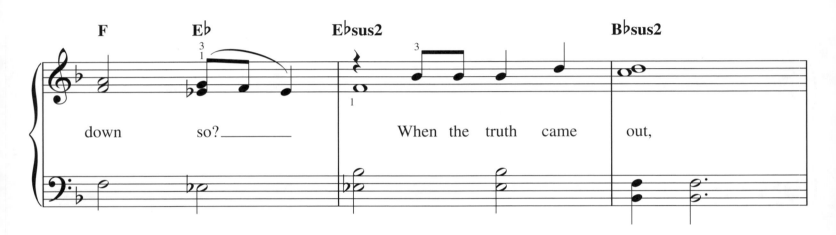

down so?_____ When the truth came out, were you the last to

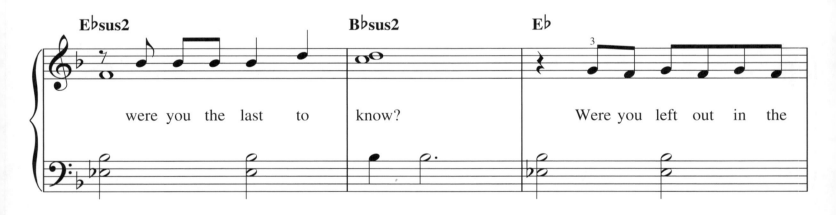

know? Were you left out in the

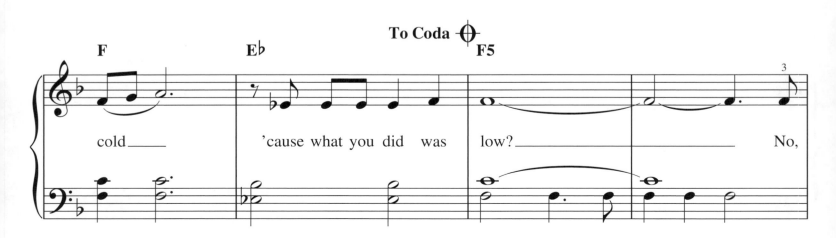

cold_____ 'cause what you did was low?_____ No,

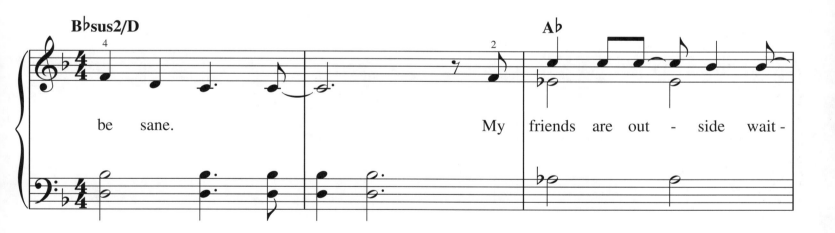

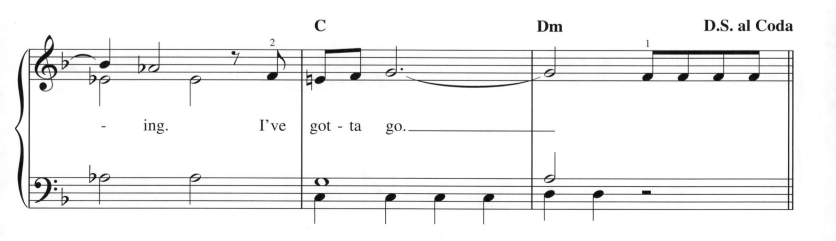

54

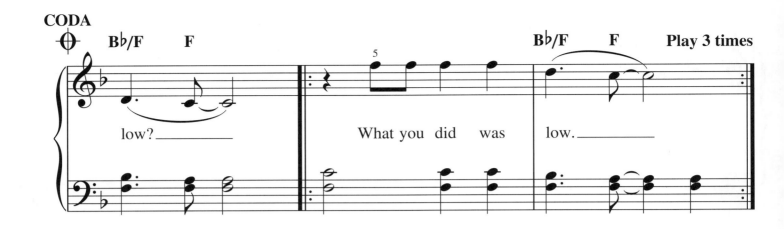

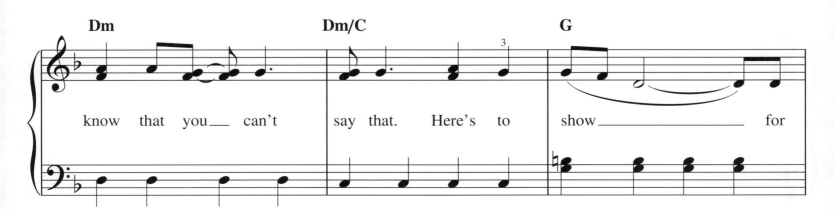

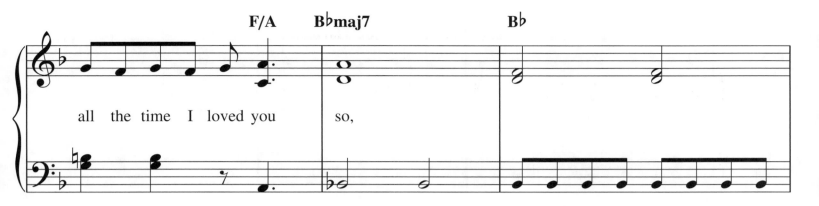

all the time I loved you so,

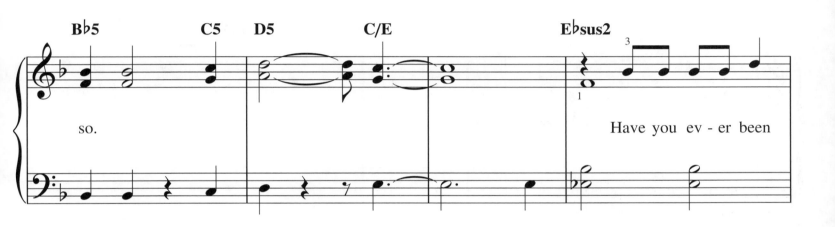

so.

Have you ev - er been

low?

Have you ev - er had a friend that let you

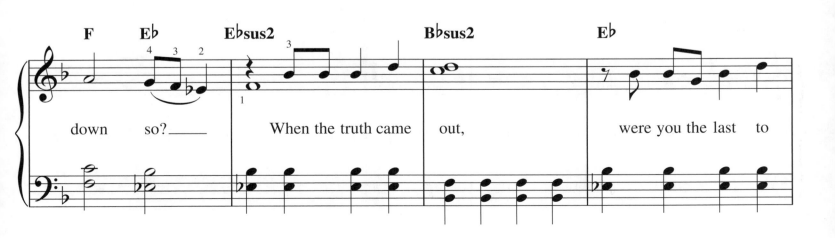

down so?_____ When the truth came out, were you the last to

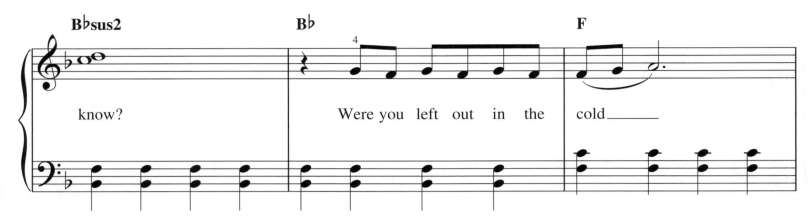

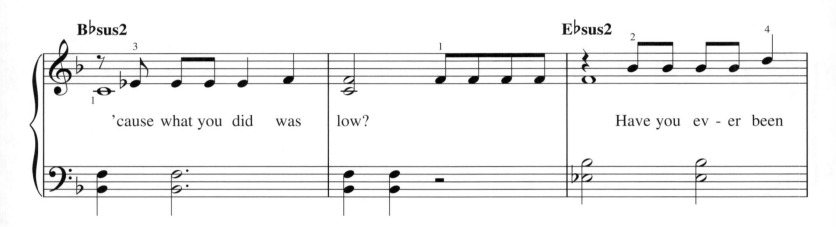

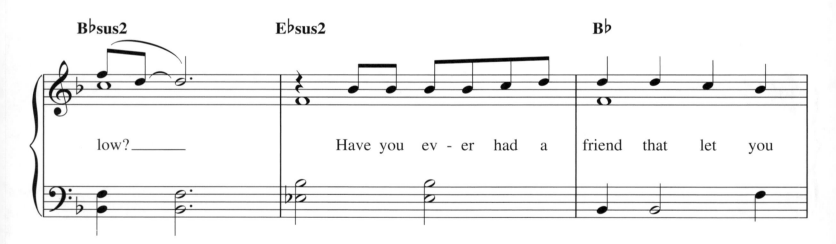

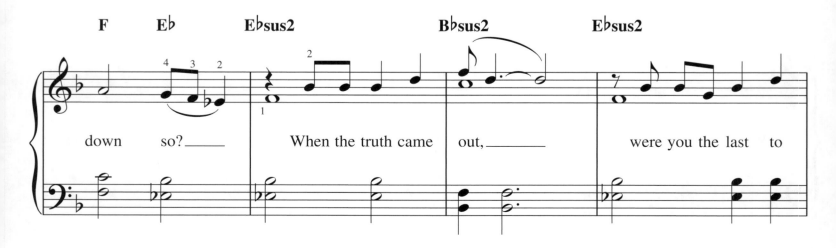

MISS INDEPENDENT

Words and Music by CHRISTINA AGUILERA, RHETT LAWRENCE,
MATTHEW MORRIS and KELLY CLARKSON

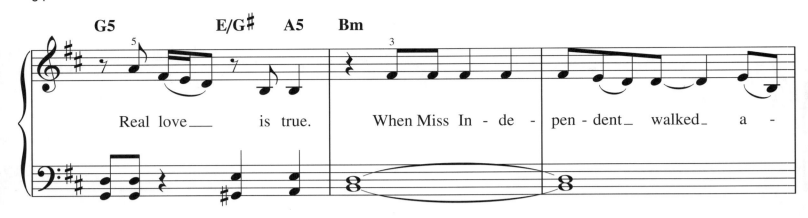

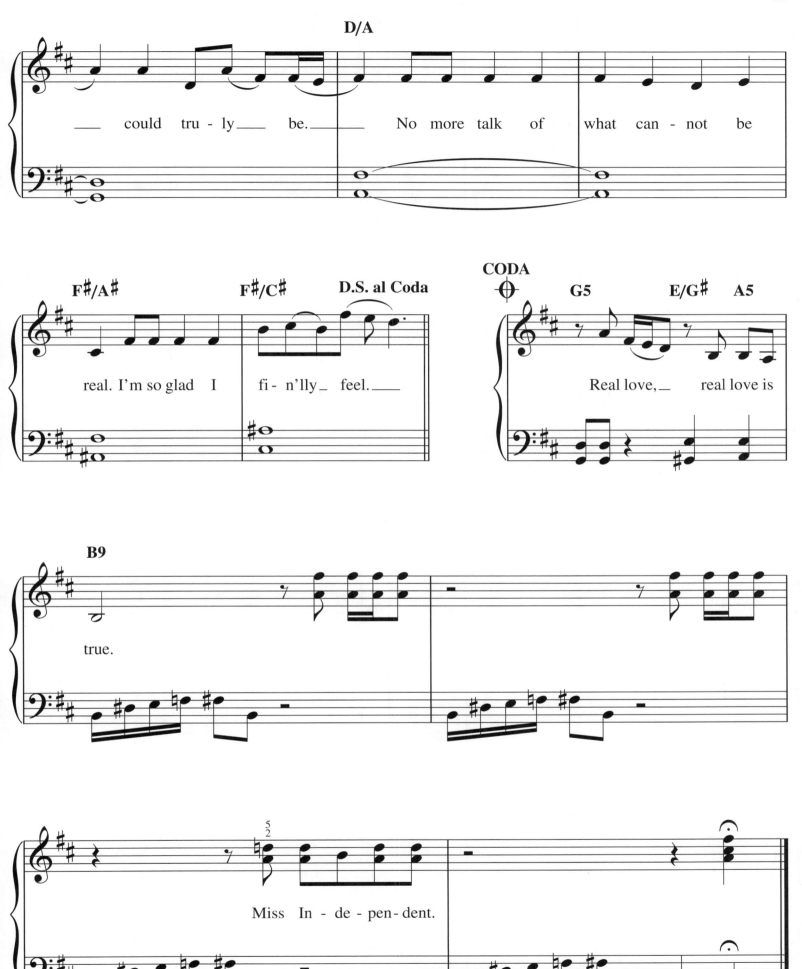

A MOMENT LIKE THIS

Words and Music by JOHN REID
and JORGEN KJELL ELOFSSON

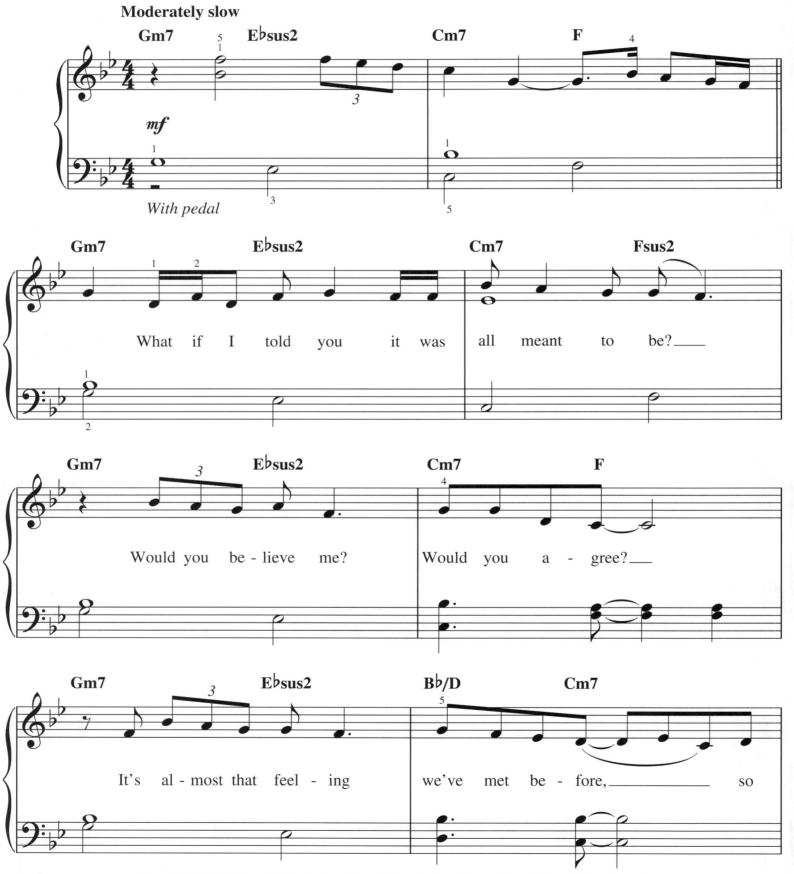

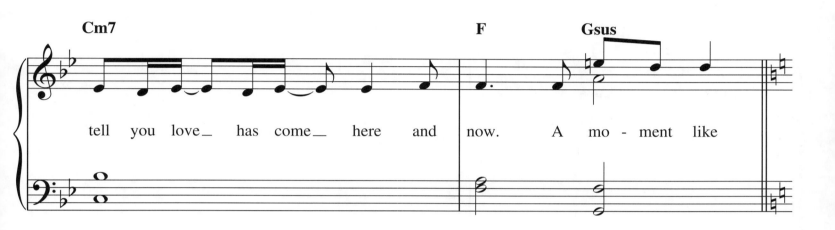

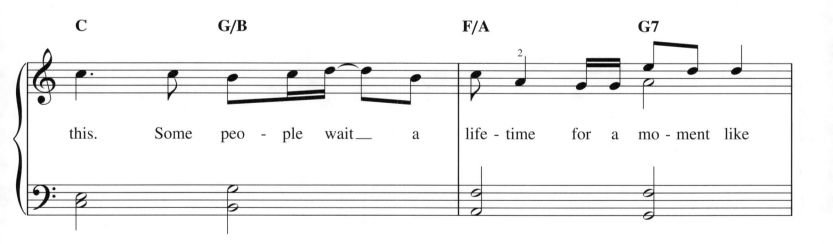

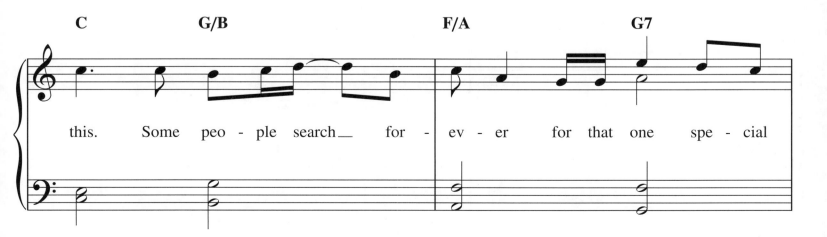

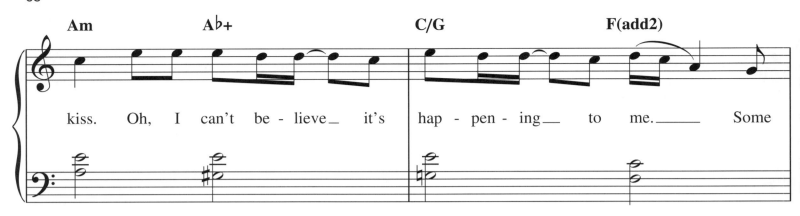

kiss. Oh, I can't be-lieve__ it's hap-pen-ing__ to me.___ Some

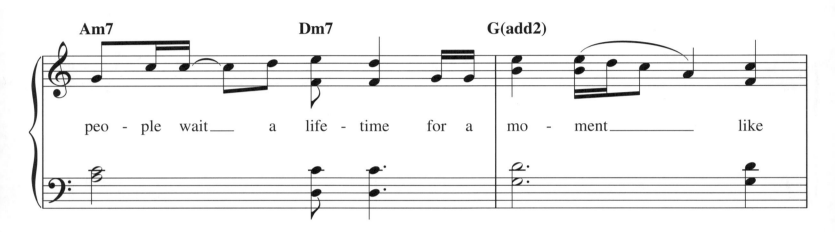

peo - ple wait__ a life - time for a mo - ment_____ like

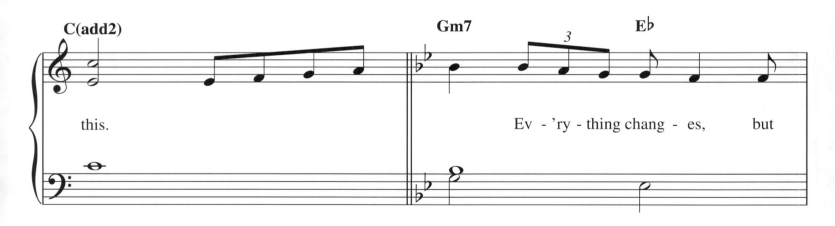

this. Ev - 'ry - thing chang - es, but

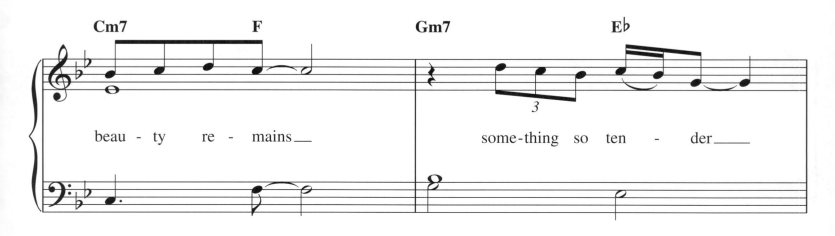

beau - ty re - mains___ some-thing so ten - der___

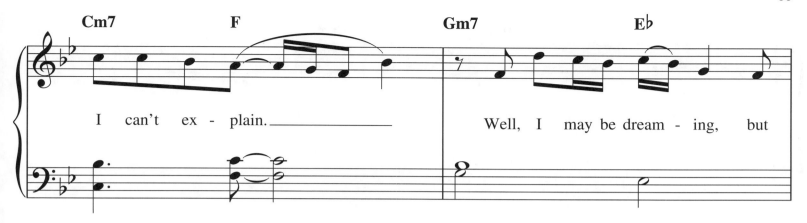

I can't ex - plain._____ Well, I may be dream - ing, but

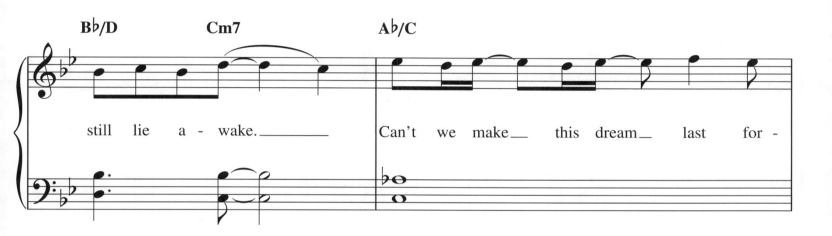

still lie a - wake._____ Can't we make__ this dream__ last for -

ev - er?__ And I'll cher - ish all__ the love_____ we

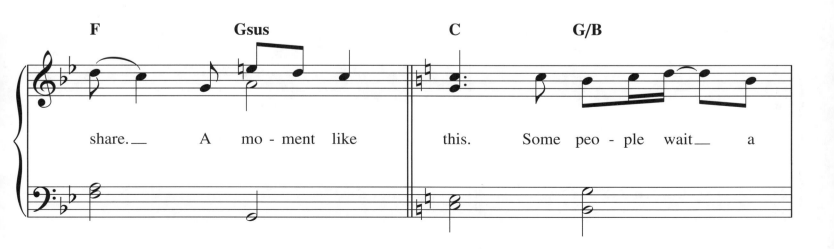

share.__ A mo - ment like this. Some peo - ple wait__ a

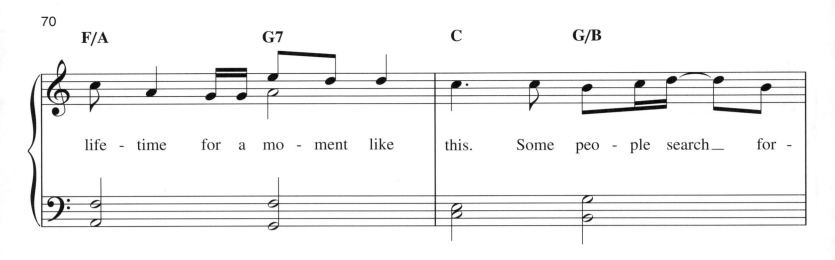

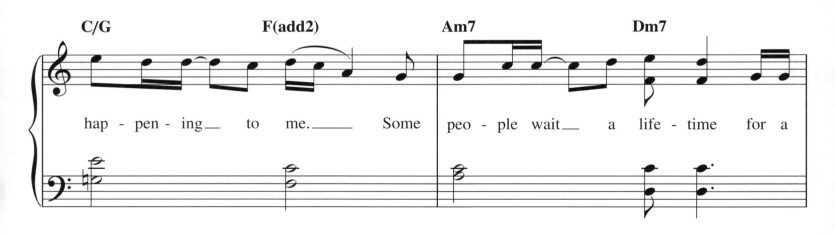

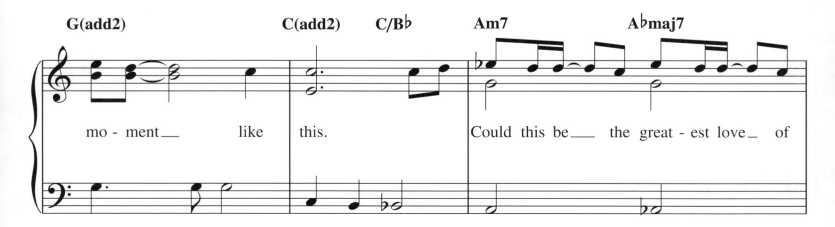

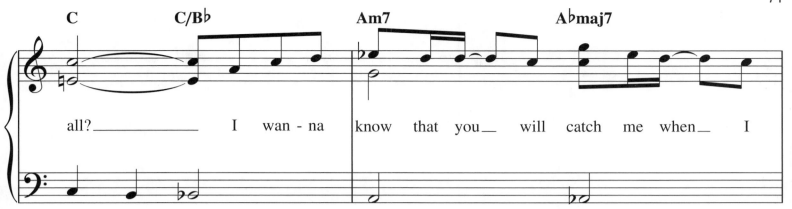

all?_____ I wan - na know that you_ will catch me when_ I

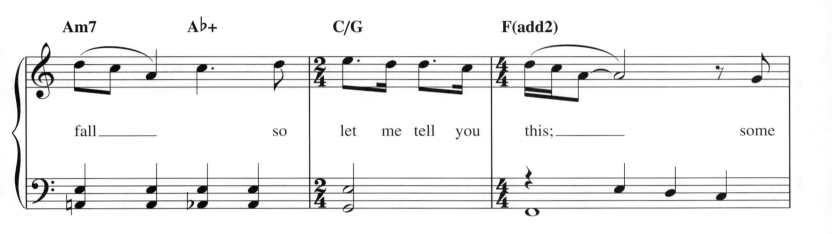

fall_____ so let me tell you this;_____ some

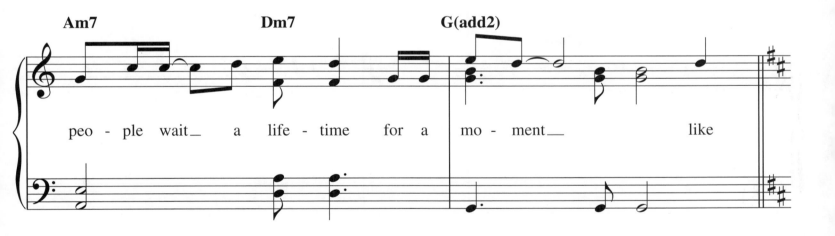

peo - ple wait_ a life - time for a mo - ment_ like

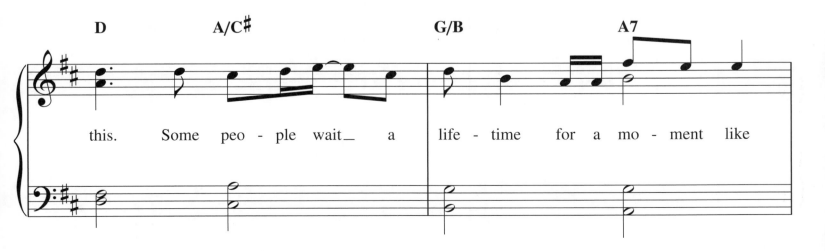

this. Some peo - ple wait_ a life - time for a mo - ment like

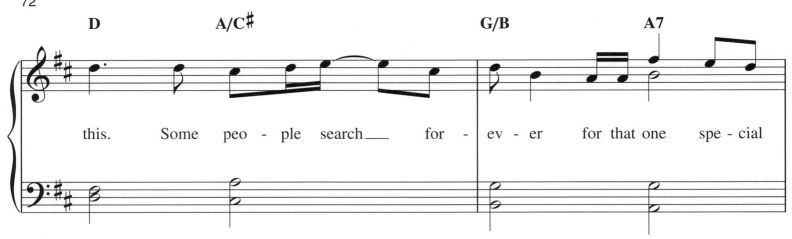

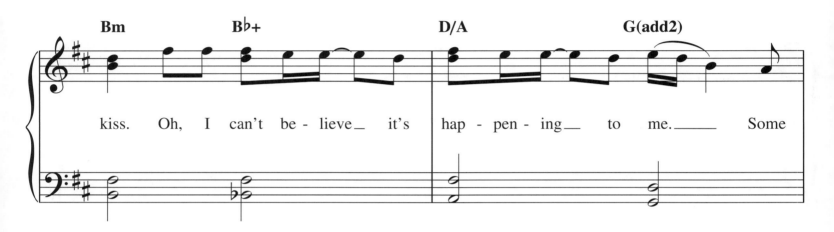

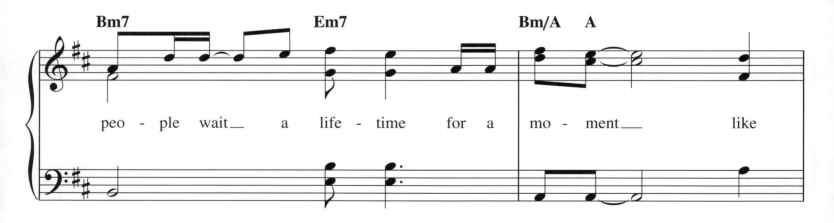

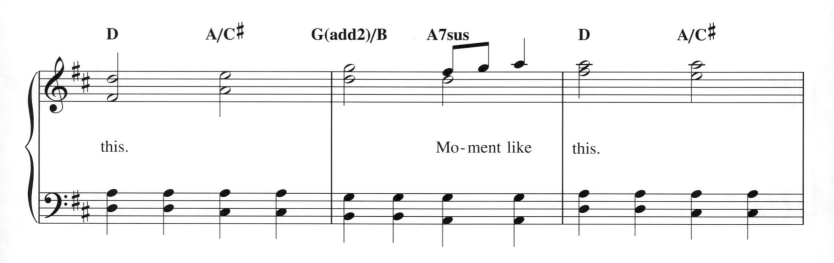

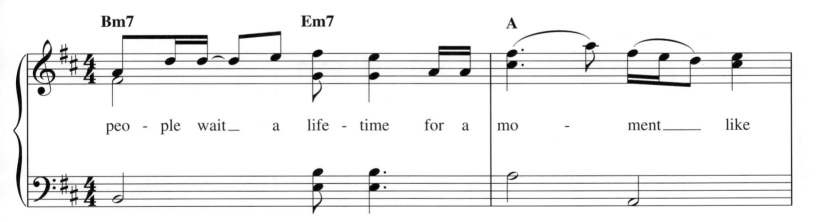

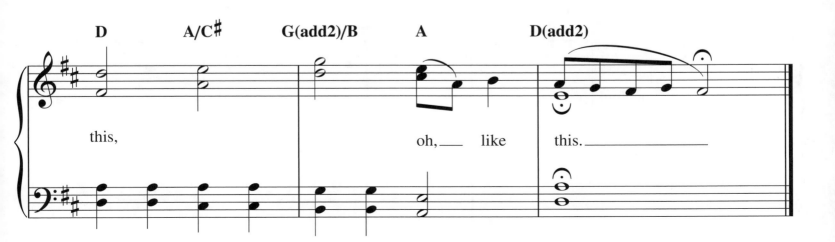

NEVER AGAIN

Words and Music by KELLY CLARKSON
and JIMMY MESSER

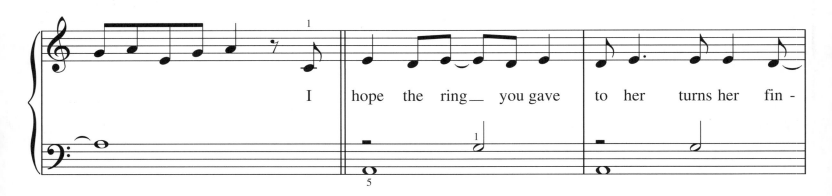

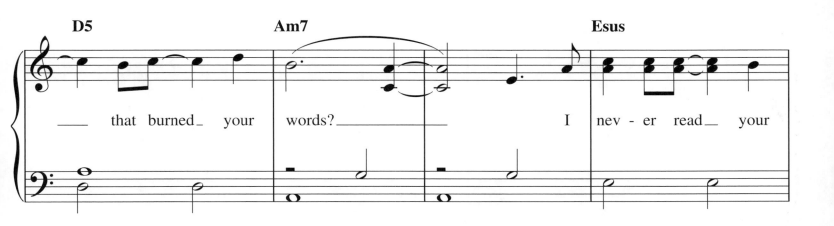

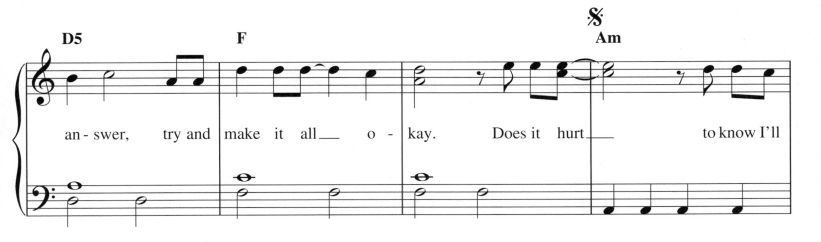

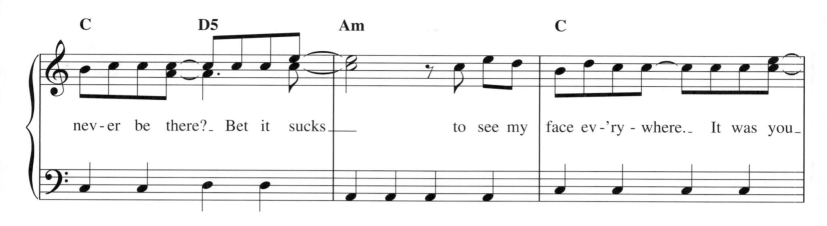

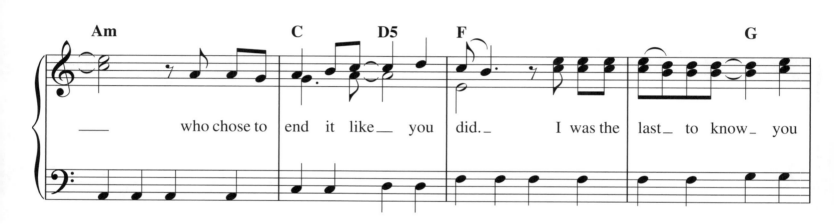

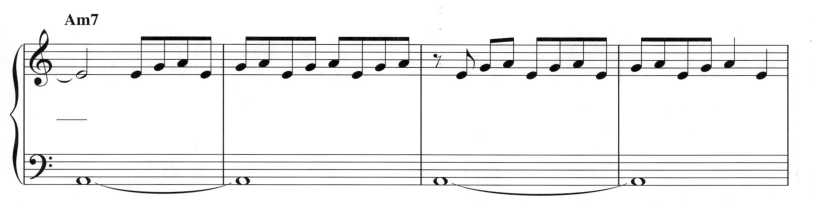

Am7

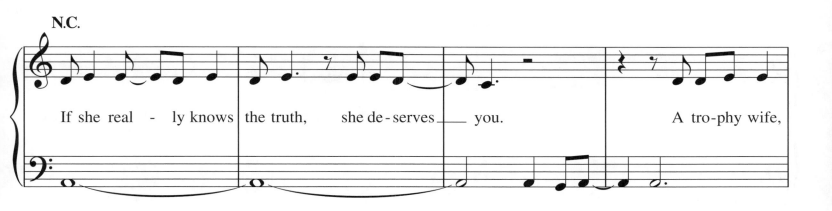

N.C.

If she real - ly knows the truth, she de - serves ___ you. A tro-phy wife,

Am7

oh, how cute. Ig - no - rance ___ is bliss. But when

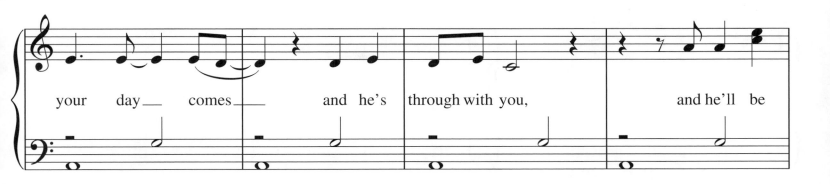

your day ___ comes ___ and he's through with you, and he'll be

through with you, you'll die to - geth - er but a - lone._____ You

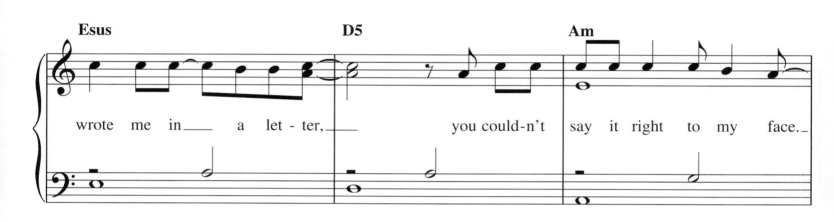

wrote me in____ a let - ter,____ you could-n't say it right to my face.__

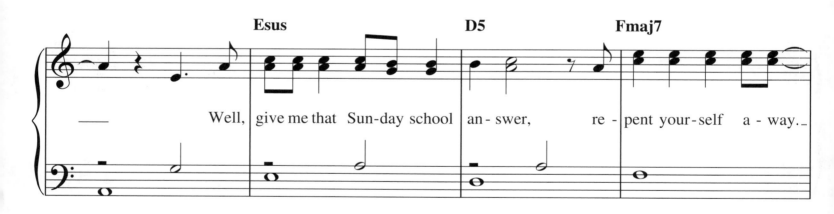

____ Well, give me that Sun-day school an - swer, re - pent your-self a - way.__

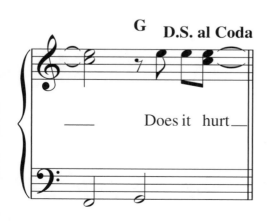

____ Does it hurt__

nev-er a - gain.__

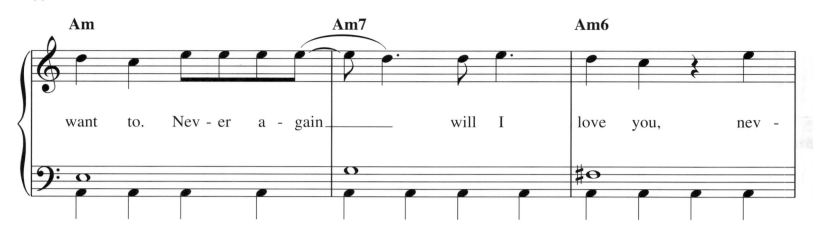

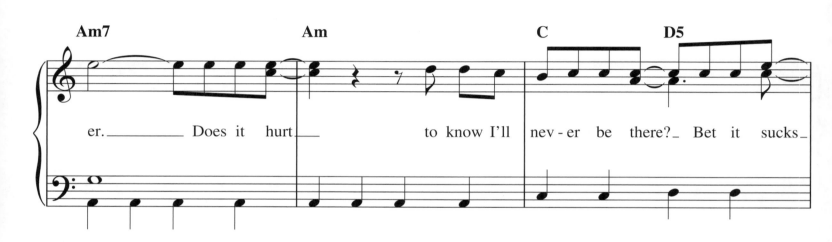

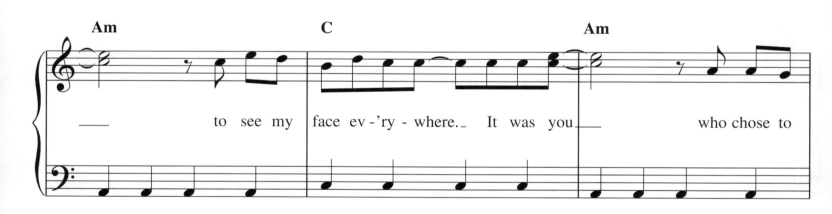

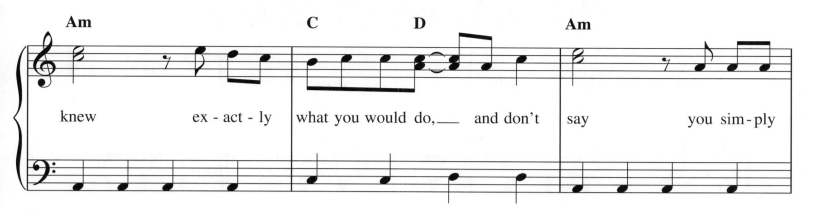

knew   ex - act - ly   what you would do,___ and don't   say   you sim-ply

lost your   way.___   They may be - lieve___ you, but I   nev - er

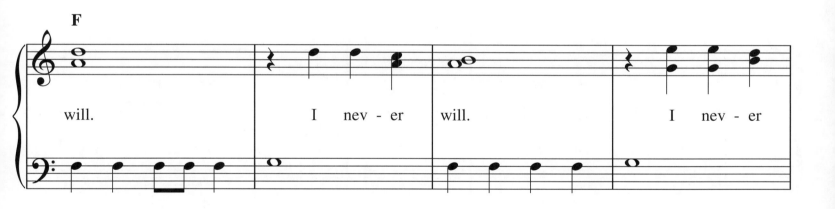

will.   I nev - er will.   I nev - er

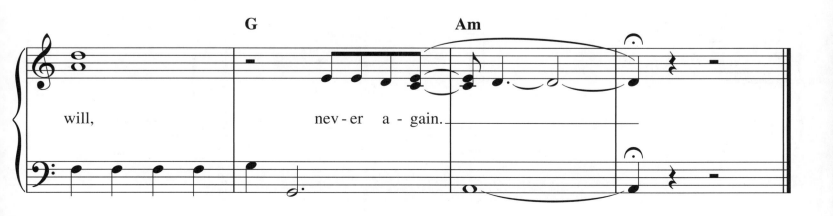

will,   nev - er a - gain.___

SINCE U BEEN GONE

Words and Music by MARTIN SANDBERG
and LUKASZ GOTTWALD

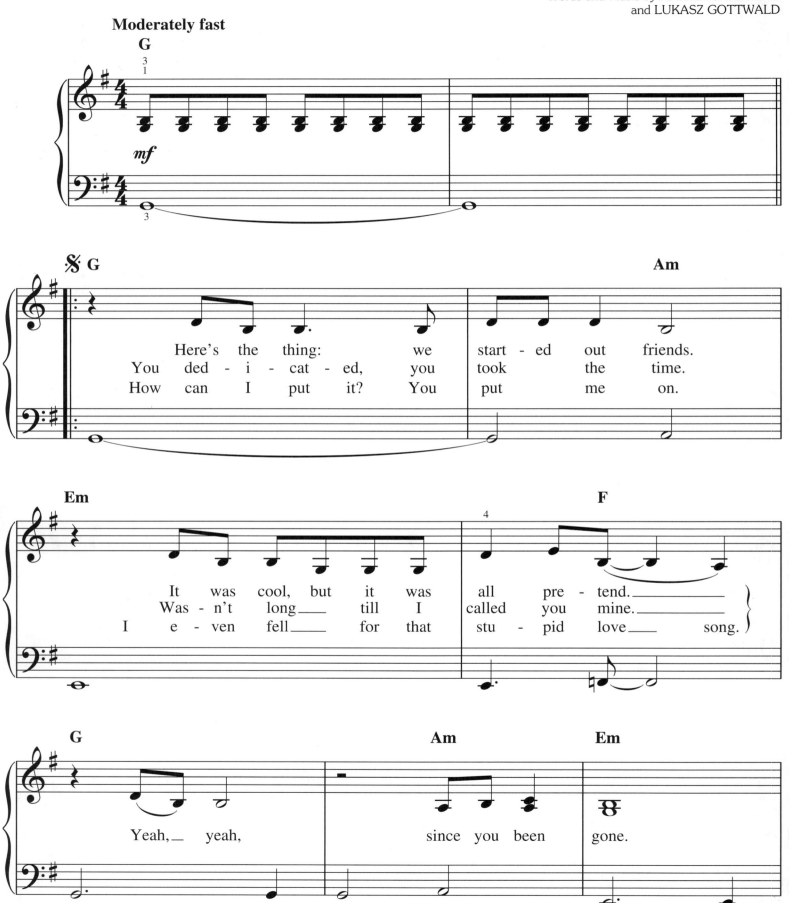

Moderately fast

Here's the thing: we start-ed out friends.
You ded-i-cat-ed, you took the time.
How can I put it? You put me on.

It was cool, but it was all pre-tend.
Was-n't long till I called you mine.
I e-ven fell for that stu-pid love song.

Yeah, yeah, since you been gone.

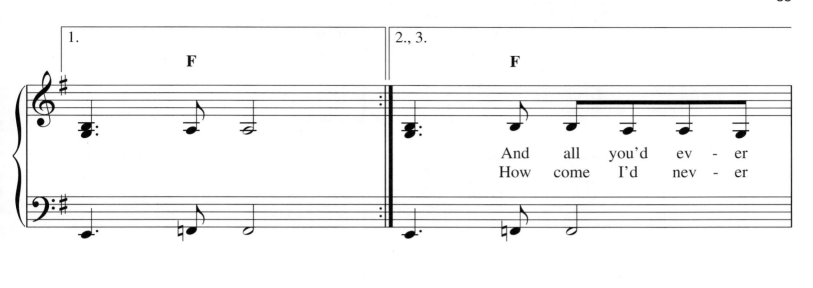

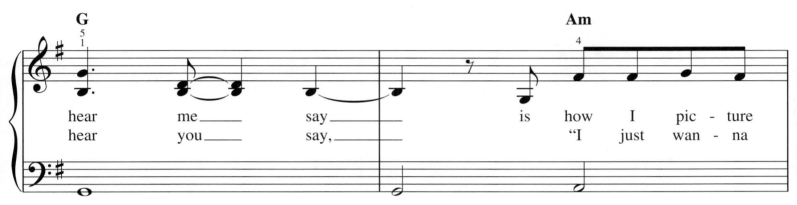

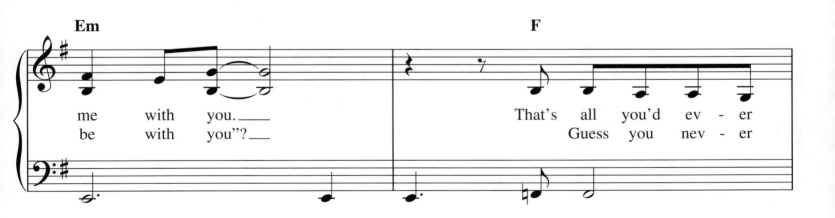

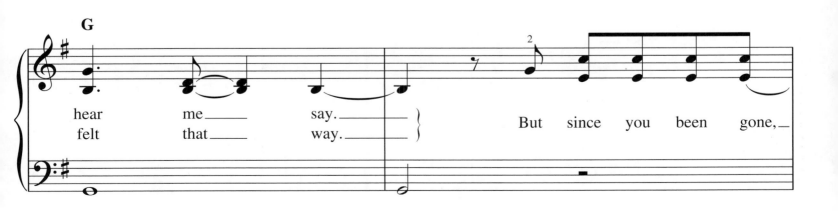

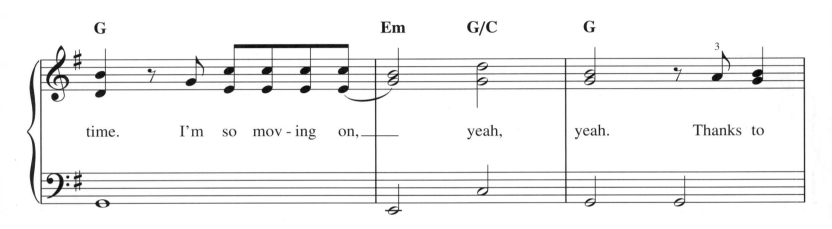

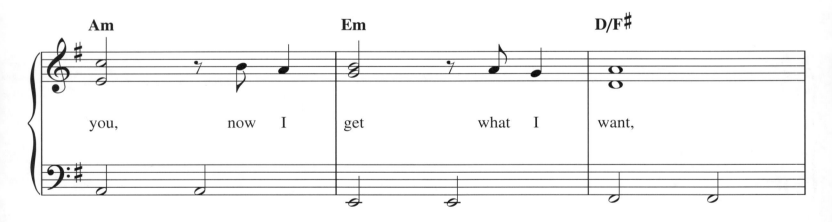

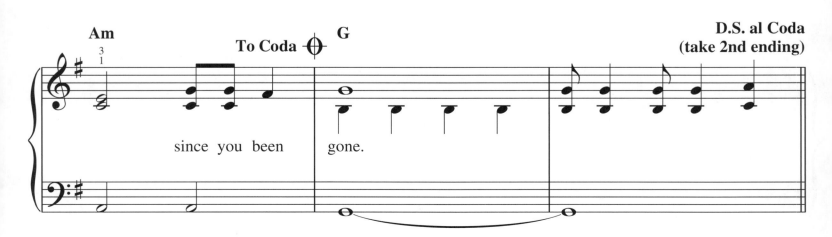

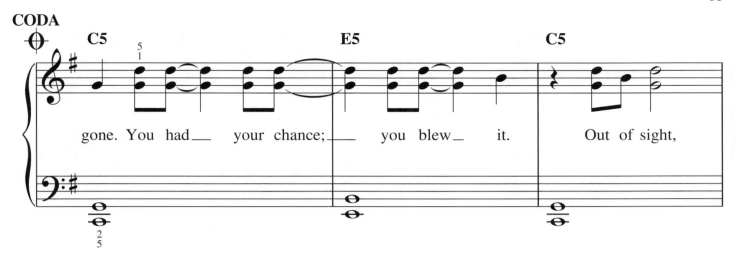

gone. You had___ your chance;___ you blew___ it.   Out of sight,

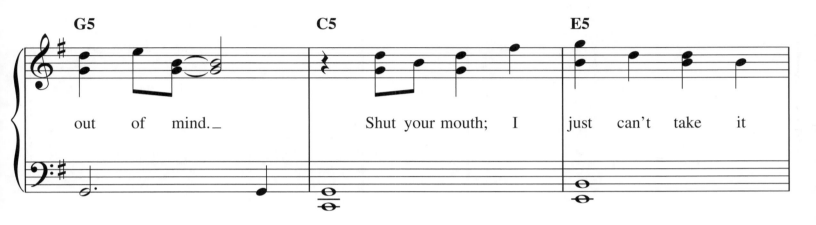

out of mind.___   Shut your mouth; I   just can't take it

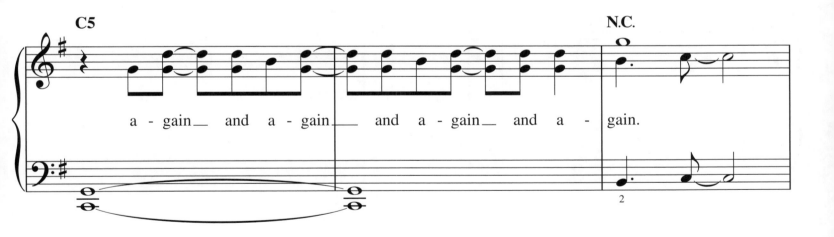

a - gain___ and a - gain___ and a - gain___ and a - gain.

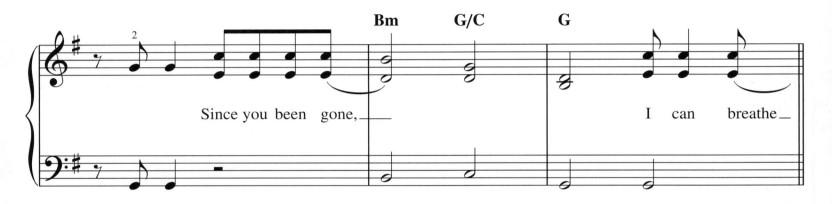

Since you been gone,＿＿ I can breathe＿

＿＿ for the first time. I'm so mov-ing on,＿＿ yeah,

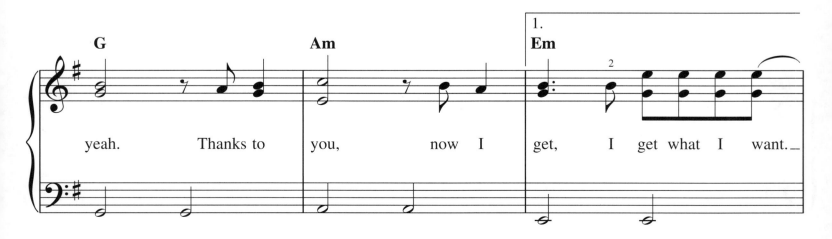

yeah. Thanks to you, now I get, I get what I want.＿

SOBER

Words and Music by KELLY CLARKSON, JIMMY MESSER,
ABEN EUBANKS and CLAMITY McENTIRE

F(add2)   **Fmaj9/C**   **F/B♭**

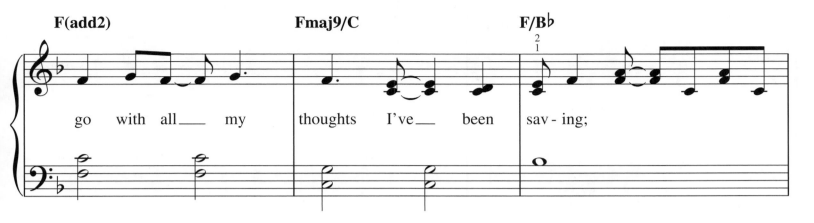

go   with   all___   my   thoughts   I've___   been   sav - ing;

Dm   **Fmaj9/C**

so   here   I   go___   with   all___   my   fears___   weigh-ing   on___

F/B♭   **Dm7**

___   me.   Three   months,_   and

F(add2)/C   **F/B♭**

I'm_____   still   so - ber;___

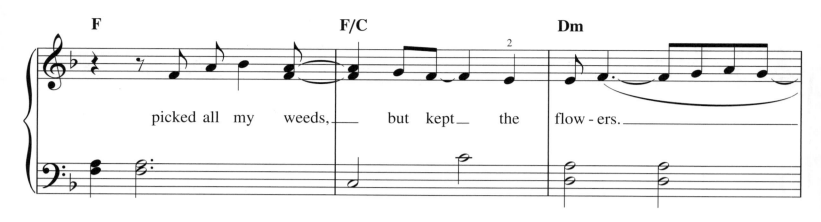

picked all my weeds, ___ but kept ___ the flow - ers. ___

___ But I know, it's nev - er real - ly

o - ver. And I don't

know; I could crash ___ and burn, ___ but

may-be   at the   end of this___ road,

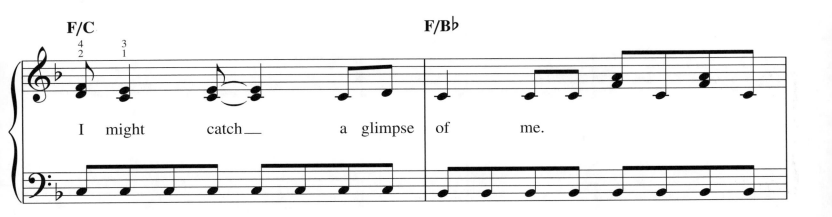

I   might   catch___   a   glimpse   of   me.

So I   won't   wor - ry 'bout___   my   tim-ing; I___ wan-na get

it right.   No   com - par-ing,   sec - ond -

guess-ing;   no,___   not   this time._____

Three   months,_   and   I'm_____   still

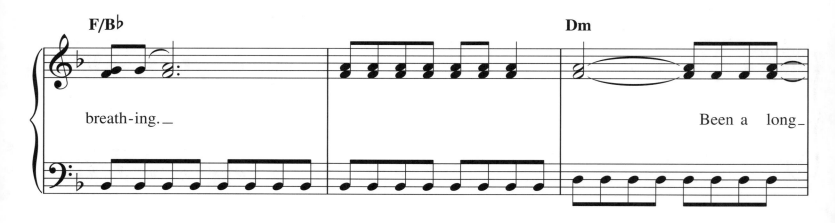

breath-ing._   Been a   long_

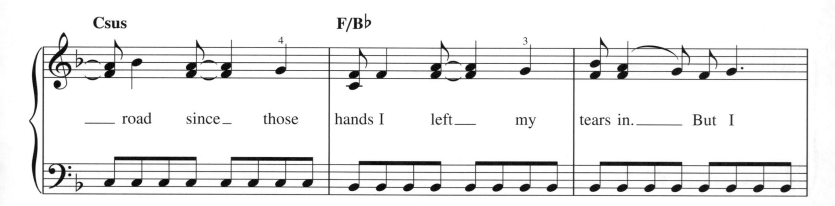

___ road   since_   those   hands I   left__   my   tears in._____ But I

know, it's nev - er real - ly o - ver,_____ no.____

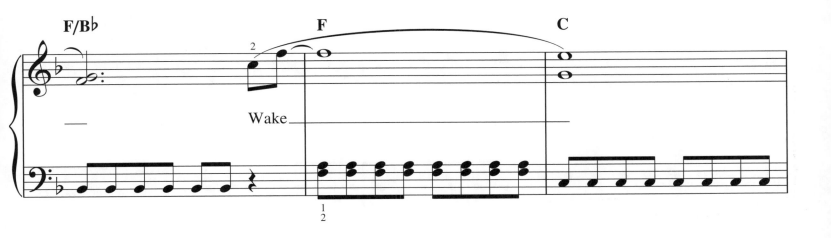

Wake_____

up... Three months,__ and

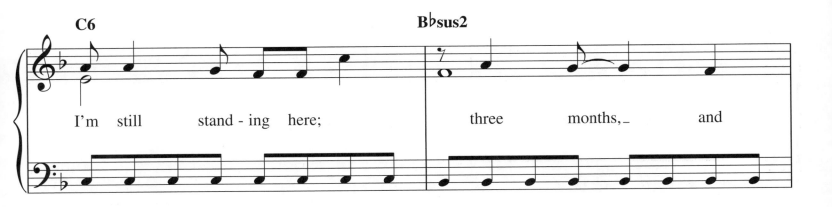

I'm still stand - ing here; three months,__ and

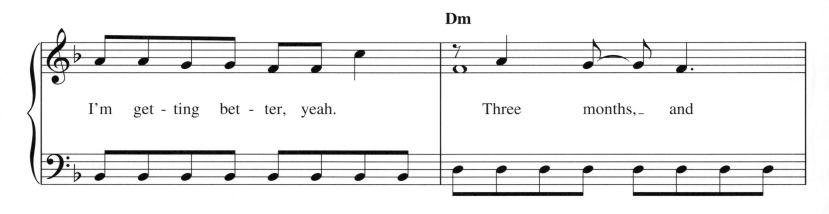

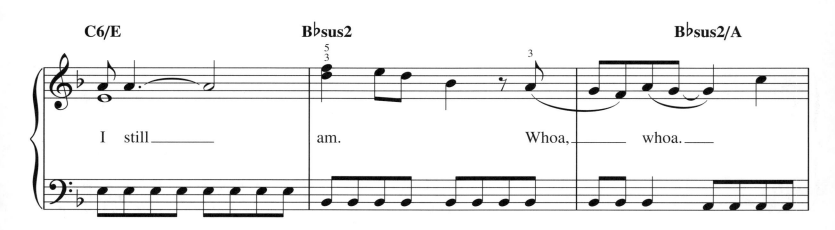

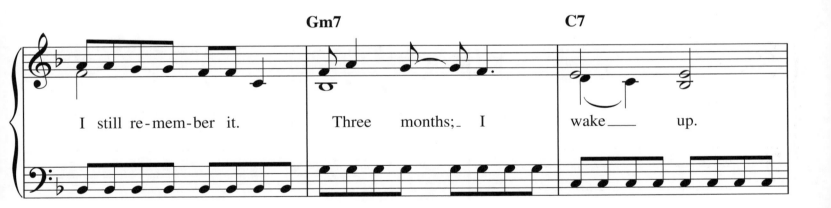

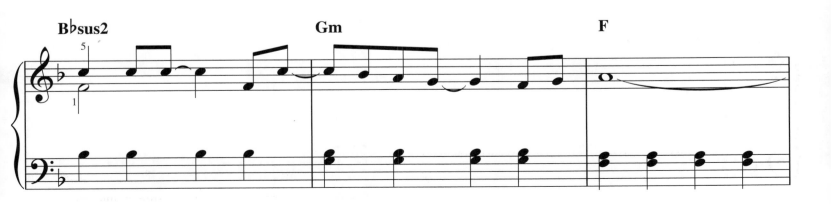

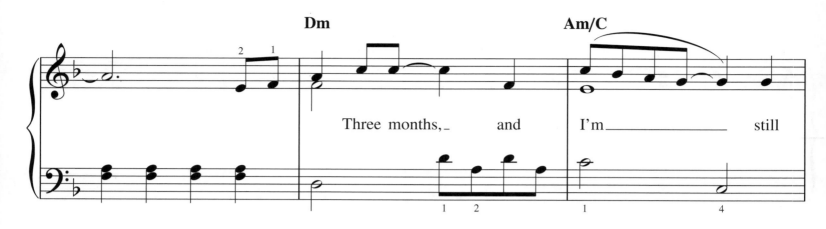

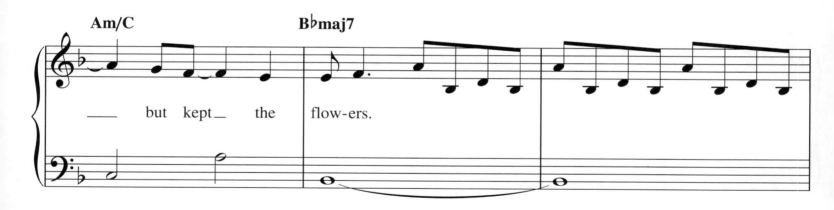

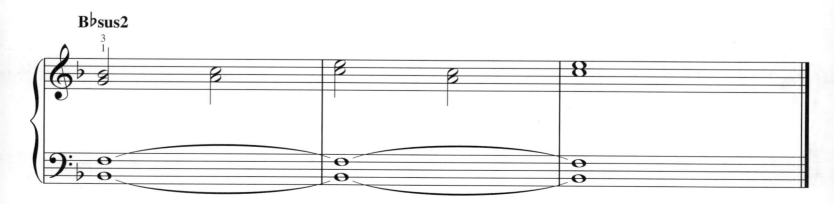

THE TROUBLE WITH LOVE IS

from LOVE ACTUALLY

Words and Music by CARL STURKEN,
EVAN ROGERS and KELLY CLARKSON

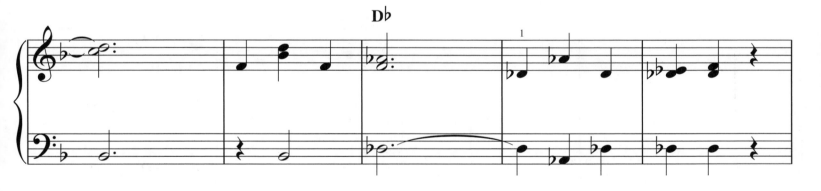

Love can be a man-y splen-dored

Now, I was once_ a_ fool,_ it's

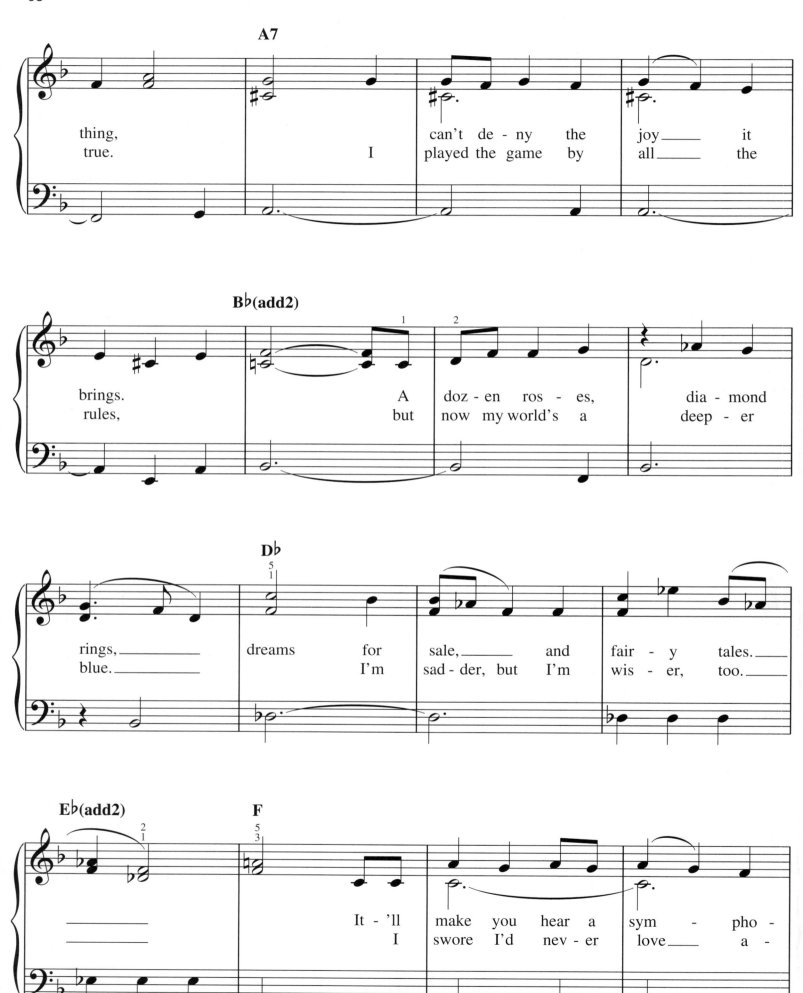

ny, and you just want the world to
gain. I swore my heart would nev - er

see._____ But like a drug that makes you
mend._____ Said love was - n't worth the

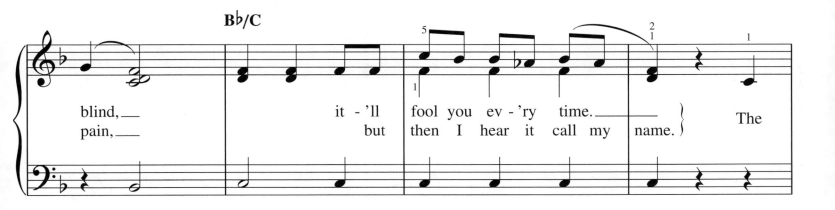

blind,_____ it - 'll fool you ev - 'ry time._____ The
pain,_____ but then I hear it call my name.

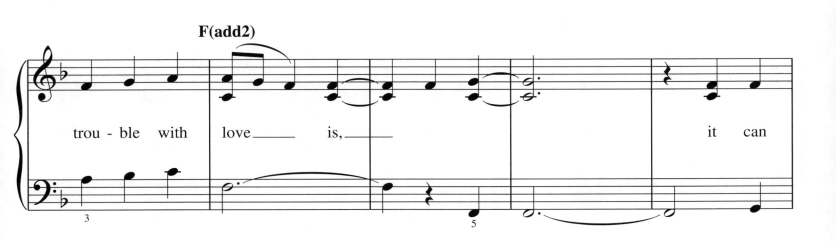

trou - ble with love_____ is,_____ it can

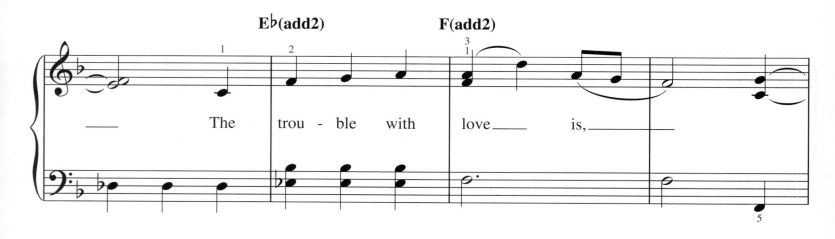

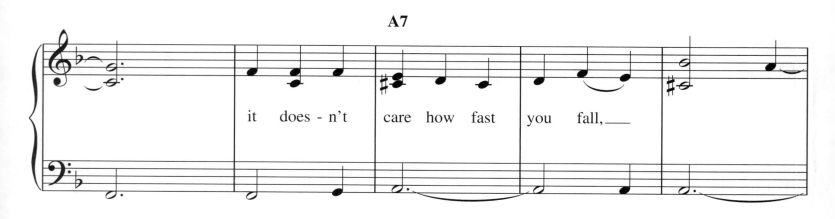

I think I've got it all fig - ured

out. My heart keeps call - in' and I keep on

fall - in', o - ver and o - ver a - gain.

This sad sto - ry al - ways ends the

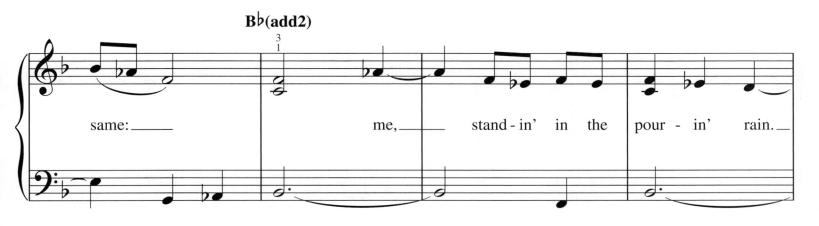

Bb(add2)

same:____ me,____ stand - in' in the pour - in' rain.__

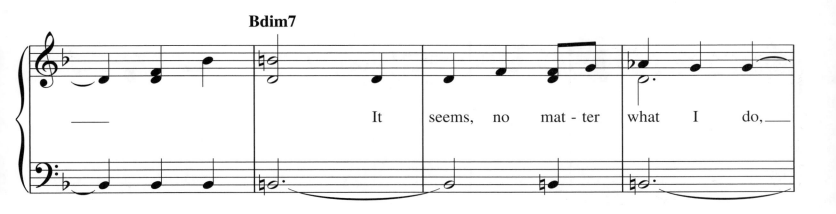

Bdim7

____ It seems, no mat - ter what I do,__

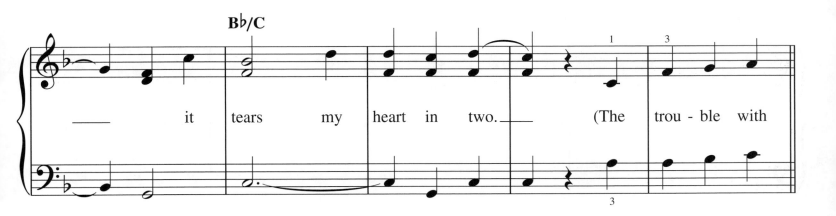

Bb/C

____ it tears my heart in two.__ (The trou - ble with

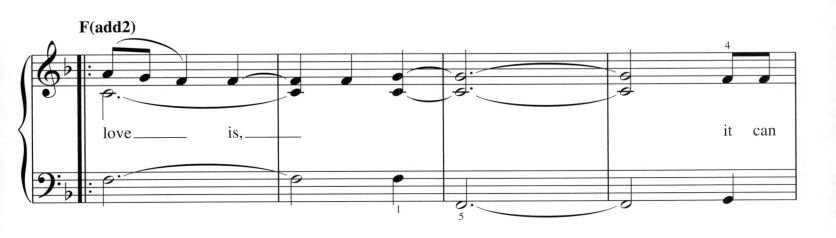

F(add2)

love____ is,____ it can

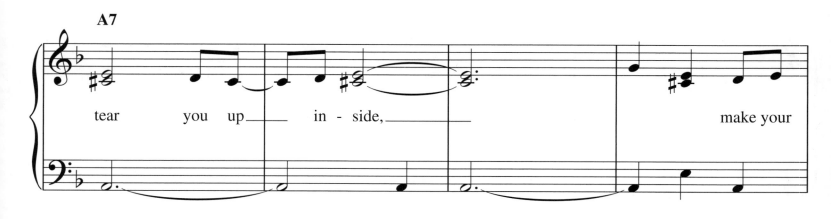

A7

tear you up___ in - side,___ make your

B♭(add2)

heart be - lieve___ a lie.)___ It's

D♭(add2)   **E♭(add2)**

strong - er than your pride.___ (The trou - ble with

F(add2)

love___ is,___ does - n't

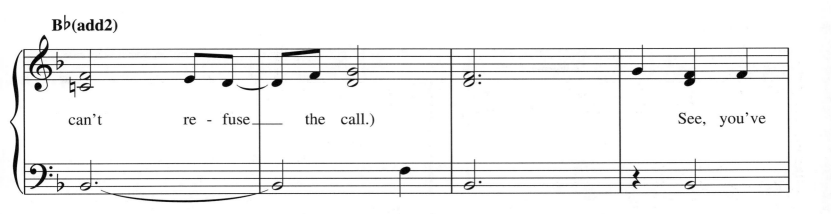

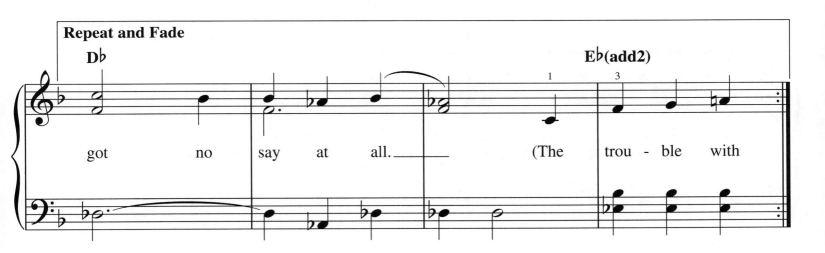

WALK AWAY

Words and Music by KELLY CLARKSON, CHANTAL KREVIAZUK,
RAINE MAIDA and KARA DioGUARDI

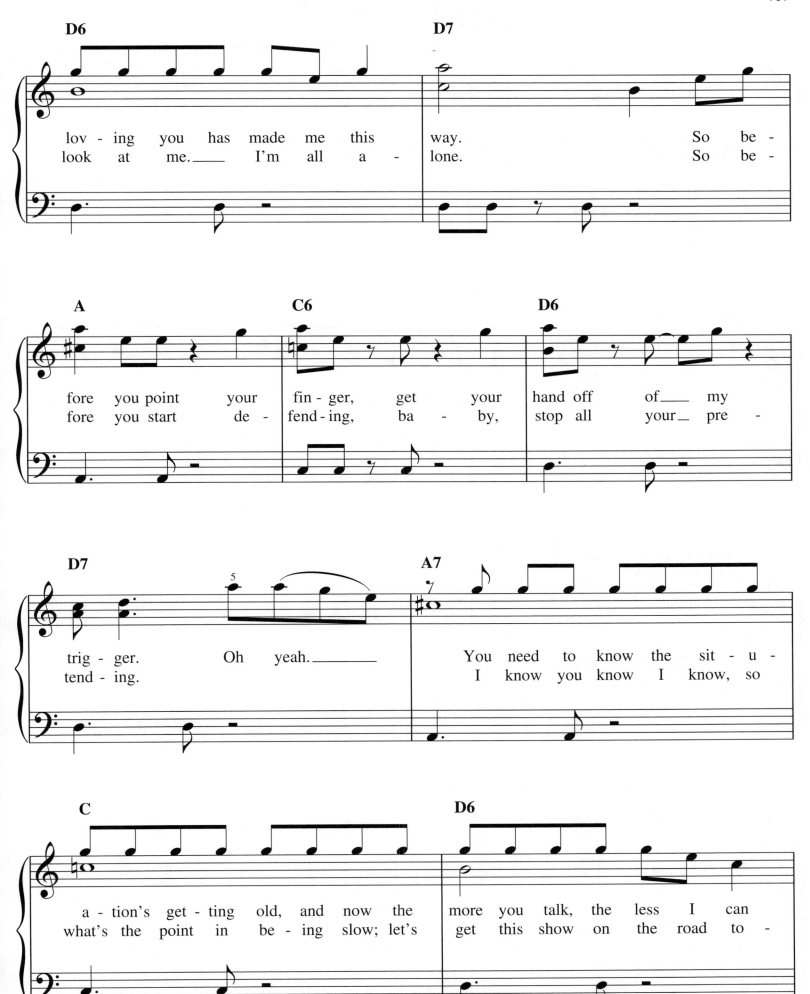

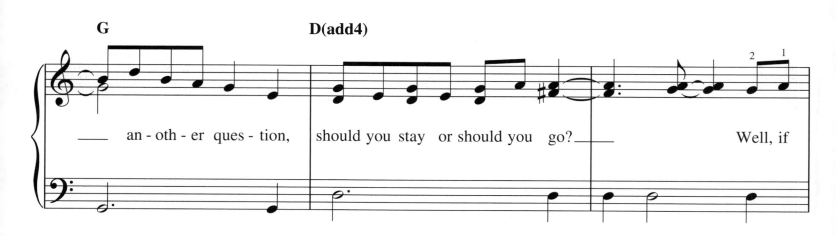

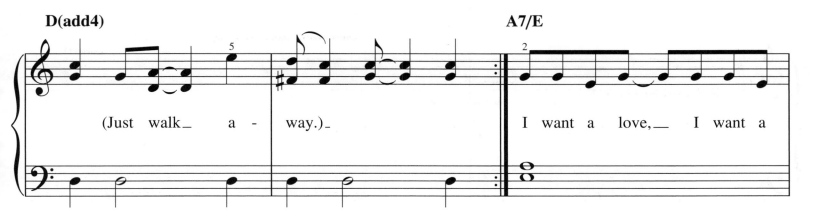

(Just walk_ a - way.)_ I want a love,__ I want a

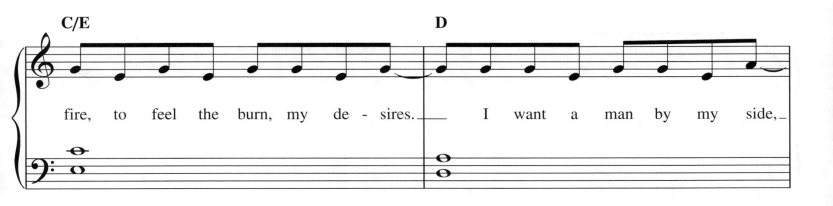

fire, to feel the burn, my de - sires.__ I want a man by my side,_

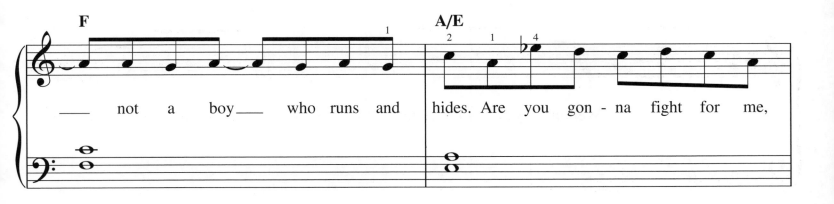

__ not a boy__ who runs and hides. Are you gon - na fight for me,

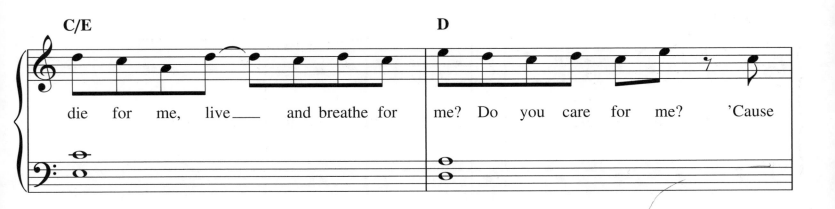

die for me, live__ and breathe for me? Do you care for me? 'Cause

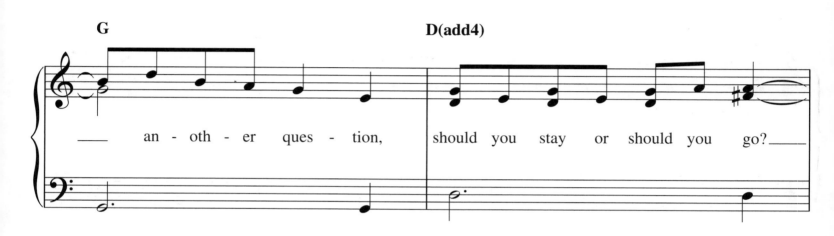

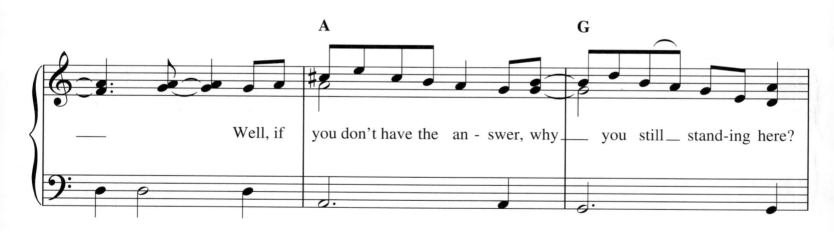

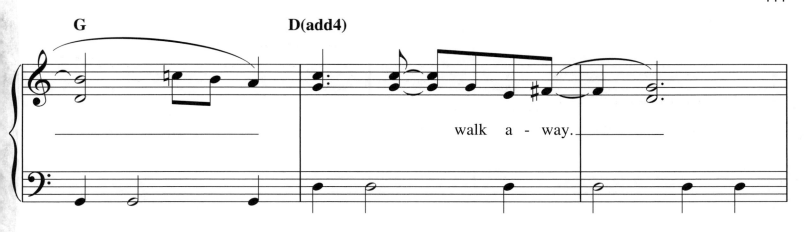

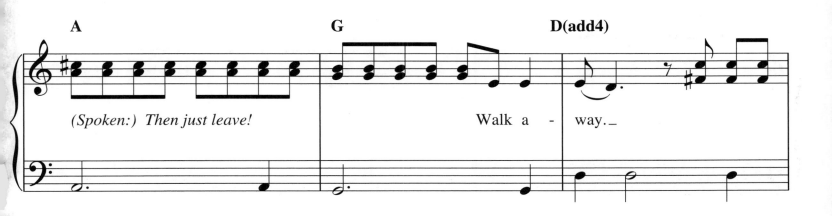

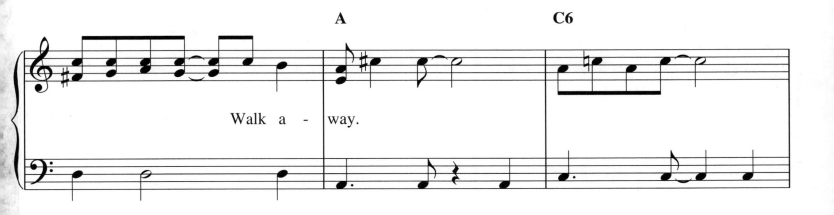